The Emotional Freedom Workbook

Take Control of Your Life and Experience Emotional Strength

Stephen Arterburn & Connie Neal

OLIVER NELSON

THOMAS NELSON PUBLISHERS
Nashville • Atlanta • London • Vancouver

Copyright © 1997 by Stephen Arterburn and Connie Neal

Published in Nashville, Tennessee, by Thomas Nelson, Inc., Publishers, and distributed in Canada by Word Communications, Ltd., Richmond, British Columbia.

Scripture quotations noted NKJV are from THE NEW KING JAMES VERSION. Copyright © 1979, 1980, 1982, Thomas Nelson, Inc., Publishers.

Scripture quotations noted NRSV are from the New Revised Standard Version of the Bible. Copyright © 1989 by the Division of Christian Education of the National Council of the Churches of Christ in the United States of America.

Scripture quotations noted NASB are from the NEW AMERICAN STANDARD BIBLE ®, © copyright The Lockman Foundation 1960, 1962, 1963, 1968, 1971, 1972, 1973, 1975, 1977. Used by permission.

Scripture quotations noted CEV are from THE CONTEMPORARY ENGLISH VERSION. © 1991 by the American Bible Society. Used by permission.

Scripture quotations noted TLB are from *The Living Bible,* copyright 1971 by Tyndale House Publishers, Wheaton, IL. Used by permission.

ISBN 0-7852-7918-0

Printed in the United States of America.
4 5 6   02 01

Contents

Introduction   *1*

My Commitment to Emotional
    Freedom   *3*
Choosing My Companion   *6*
Finding a Support Group   *11*

Part 1: Shame

Healthy and Unhealthy Shame   *16*
Identifying the Symptoms
    of Shame   *21*
Shame and Addictions   *24*
Setting Goals for Getting Rid
    of Shame   *28*
Clearing Away Legitimate Guilt   *31*
Finding Your Sources of Shame   *35*
That's What Friends Are For   *40*
Drawing Close to Those Who
    Lessen Your Shame   *46*
Know the Real God   *49*
Making Changes   *53*
Finding a New Audience   *57*
Look for Seeds of Potential   *60*
Acquiring Knowledge and Skills to Help
    You Fit In   *62*
Developing Your Unique Talents
    and Abilities   *66*
Finding Fulfillment in Your Work   *69*
Coping with Weaknesses   *71*
Adopting New Rituals and
    Symbols   *75*
Treating Yourself with Respect   *77*

Part 2: Unhealthy Relationships

What Is Codependency?   *81*
The Tree of Your Life   *84*
Gaining Power   *88*
Pruning Back Unhealthy Relational
    Patterns   *91*
The Focus Is on You   *95*
Inner Versus Outward
    Direction   *99*
Finding the Missing Pieces   *102*
Take a Look at Your Physical
    Life   *105*
Take a Look at Your Emotional
    Life   *110*
What Do You Believe About Yourself?
    115
Mental, Spiritual, and Financial Warning
    Signs   *119*
Rediscovering Talents, Treasures, and
    Dreams   *127*
Accepting Full Responsibility for Your
    Life   *131*
Facing Your Fears   *135*
Establishing Relationship
    Boundaries   *138*
Dealing with the Past   *143*
Sorting Out Obstacles and
    Injuries   *146*
Using Your Strength Wisely   *150*

Part 3: Depression

Finding Motivation (When You Don't
Feel Like Moving)   155
Your Path Will Be Unique   159
Dealing with Your Addictions   162
The Progression Out of the Pit   165
Taking Care of Your Physical
Health   168
Nurturing a Healthy Mind   171
Nourishing Your Spiritual Health   174
Strengthening Relationships That Lift
You Up   179
Are You Dealing with Normal
Depression?   184
Are You Dealing with a Depressive
Illness?   190
Are You Dealing with Negative
Attitudes and Beliefs?   196
Are You Dealing with Spiritual or
Relational Issues?   204
Unraveling a Mystery Depression   209
Creating Your Personal Treatment and
Recovery Plan   212
Setting Boundaries to Uphold Your
Happiness   214
Accepting Full Responsibility for Your
Life Again   217
Appreciating the Value of Sorrow
and Pain   219

Part 4: Procrastination

Are You a Procrastinator?   224
Procrastination Serves Your
Purposes   228

Learning to Choose   230
Give Yourself Some Slack   233
Neglect, Avoidance, or Refusal?   236
Streamlining Your Life   238
Confused or Conflicting Priorities   241
Time Out: Overcommitted and
Undernourished   244
The Problem of Pain   246
Avoiding Embarrassment and
Shame   248
Fear of Failure, Fear of Success   250
Monsters in the Dark: Fear of the
Unknown   254
The Silent Power of
Procrastination   256
Promising to Please: Thinking No
But Saying Yes   258
Overwhelmed by Reality   261
Dealing with Procrastination One
Day at a Time   264
The Realm of What's Okay   266
Making Friends with Failure   268
Finding Your Success Comfort
Zone   271
Scheduling and Your Personal
Boundaries   273
Making Amends   276

Celebrating Your Success   279
About the Authors   283

Introduction

*E**motional freedom*. It sounds like a wonderful goal, doesn't it? But what does it really mean? We define *emotional freedom* as the "ability to live life to the fullest without being hindered by emotional difficulties."

Negative feelings often get in the way of our best intentions. We want to accomplish something. We consider the possibilities, make plans, and take preliminary steps in the direction of that goal. But just when we think we're on our way, things start going wrong. We find ourselves slowing down. Getting stuck. Before long, we realize we're going nowhere.

It isn't our minds that stop us—mentally, we know what we want, and we usually know how to get there.

It isn't our bodies that get in the way, either—most of us are in reasonably good health.

When our dreams get derailed, the culprit is usually found hiding in the emotional life. It is a pattern of attitudes, habits, or relationships that won't allow us to move forward, no matter how much we tell ourselves we want to.

In the following pages, we'll be working through emotional obstacles that are all too familiar to most of us:

- Shame—because it locks us into our past
- Unhealthy relationships—because they distract us from our unique purpose in life
- Depression—because we have not grieved our sorrows
- Procrastination—because we are afraid to try

These emotional traps capture each of us in different ways. And they often overlap. But chances are, all of them have slowed you down at one time or another. And some of them may have locked you up for years.

As we begin our journey, you must not overlook some spiritual concerns. First and foremost, it is essential for you to acknowledge that you can change your life only with God's help. His power, not yours, is your hope for the future. Confess your sins and shortcomings to him, and turn away from your wrong behaviors. As you take responsibility for the things you've done wrong, you'll need to ask for forgiveness from some people and offer forgiveness to other people. Ask them, if necessary, to forgive you. From there, you can move forward into the specific issues that keep you locked up in emotional bondage.

Since freedom is the goal, we encourage you to feel free to start working through this book at the beginning of any one of the four parts. Think about each of the four subjects, and decide where you would like to focus your work.

However, once you've started a part, I strongly advise you to finish it. The workbook process has been carefully designed to lead you step-by-step on an exciting spiritual pilgrimage toward greater emotional health.

Feel free to work at your own pace, if at all possible, with a partner who will support you in your efforts. And please—take enough time to reflect on each activity, to tell yourself the truth, and to enjoy the sense of discovery you'll experience as you move forward—toward *emotional freedom*.

My Commitment to Emotional Freedom

What you commit yourself to become determines what you are.
—Tony Campolo

Your journey to emotional freedom requires a firm commitment. If your life is in bondage to shame, unhealthy relationships, depression, procrastination, or any other unhealthy pattern of behavior, you know change is necessary. But to achieve that change, you will have to decide that change is a priority, and that you are committed to doing what is necessary to attain emotional freedom.

Your commitment will mark the beginning of a confrontation with your captors. It will lead you in the direction of your deepest fears and, along the way, you may uncover areas of pain that you have not yet dealt with. To begin the journey toward emotional freedom, you will need a glimmer of hope, a tiny spark of faith, and a fair amount of courage. You will put all of them into action through your determined commitment to complete your search for happiness, fulfillment, healthy family relationships, a degree of intimacy that will allow you to give and receive true love, a reasonable measure of success, satisfying friendships, and peace with yourself.

Faith and hope are always essential. But courage is particularly important to you. Courage is not, of course, an absence of fear. Courage is determining to use your strength and resources to take steps in the right direction, even if you are afraid. More important, you can draw courage from a loving God who will never leave you in the midst of life's battles. You can also draw courage from others who have overcome their emotional bondage to discover a wealth of freedom beyond. You can draw courage from people who love you and believe the best of you. So summon your faith and hope. Gather up all the courage within your reach. And determine to make a firm commitment to complete the journey into emotional freedom.

Take a moment to reflect on the following questions, then write your answers.

1. What dream causes you to desire emotional freedom? _____
_____
_____

2. Who or what will be the source (or sources) of your courage to keep moving forward? _____
_____

3. Are you willing to make a commitment to yourself to complete this process? If you are hesitant, explain why. _____
_____
_____

4. If you are uncertain about making a solid commitment, what feelings accompany your uncertainty? Anger? Defensiveness? Fear? Sadness?
_____
_____

5. What are three strong reasons you should move forward anyway?
_____
_____

MY COMMITMENT TO EMOTIONAL FREEDOM

After answering the five questions, carefully read the following commitment. When you are ready to do so, prayerfully sign it, asking God to help you keep it.

I, _____, am serious about my desire to attain emotional freedom. I want to be able to go where I long to go, do what I want to do, and be who I truly am with a sense of dignity and self-respect.

Until I complete *The Emotional Freedom Workbook,* I will invest the time to read a passage each day and reserve thirty minutes of quiet time to reflect on the issues addressed. I plan to take this time each (*circle one*) morning, lunchtime, afternoon, evening, or before bedtime. I will honestly consider the questions before I answer them, and I will also journal my feelings as truthfully as possible. I will share this journey with someone I trust; I will make myself accountable to this person to complete the journey, and I will look to this person for encouragement.

I understand that to reach this goal, I must be willing to exercise the courage to look at myself carefully and to endeavor to meet all challenges with perseverance.

I am willing to move toward truth, even if it is upsetting, and to look back to gain a new perspective from which I can move forward to a better life. I am willing to reexamine my beliefs about myself, my way of life, and my relationships to make changes that can give me emotional freedom.

I make this commitment to myself this _____ day of _____, _____.

Signed _____

Choosing My Companion

Two are better than one, because they have a good reward for their toil. For if they fall, one will lift up the other; but woe to one who is alone and falls and does not have another to help.—*Ecclesiastes 4:9–10* NRSV

The path of emotional bondage is sometimes a lonely one. You may be surrounded by others, but only superficially. You do not allow them into the inner chambers of your life. You fear that they will discover the "truth" about you, and in knowing you, they will hurt you or you will hurt them.

You sometimes isolate yourself from the people you care most about. You drive them away because you believe that their involvement with you would bring them to ultimate ruin. Because of the way you see yourself, you consider this a caring act; you are protecting them from the pain you believe is inherent in a relationship with someone as flawed as you are.

You also tend to keep people away to protect yourself. You don't want to risk the rejection of those whose love you desire the most. You may act out your anger at being rejected by becoming hostile toward others. You may behave in socially unacceptable ways as a dare to find out if anyone will see beyond the bluster to find something lovable in you—something you aren't convinced is there. You may keep them at a distance by resorting to offensive behavior, by brandishing the shield of anger or rage, by attacking them, or by rejecting them

CHOOSING MY COMPANION

first before they have the chance to reject you. Sometimes you simply run away and make yourself unavailable.

You may keep those you care about most at a distance from "the real you" by pretending to be whoever you think they want you to be. You start out hoping that they will accept the mask you wear and love you for it, but even if they do love you on those terms, you cannot receive the love. You are left isolated, hiding within the walls of the image you present. You may give beyond the call of duty without ever giving them access to the real person hidden within. You may end up angry and resentful because you have to keep up the act to receive their love, or you may go through the motions of having a love relationship without ever being known. If so, you have isolated yourself, although they may never know it.

Reflect for a moment on your way of keeping people from really knowing you.

Sometimes I act _____
because I'm afraid to let people know that I'm _____
_____.

For example, with _____, I _____
_____.

Write your responses to the following questions:

How do you feel about sharing your journey toward emotional freedom with someone else? _____
_____

Are you fortunate to have a circle of support persons so that identifying a companion will be fairly easy? _____
_____

If you aren't able to find a companion today, are you willing to keep trying?

_____

How do you feel about looking to God for additional support as you continue your journey?_____

_____

What is your emotional reaction when you consider the possibility of telling someone your secrets? _____

_____

What do you fear will happen? _____

_____

Because you will be sharing personal secrets with this companion, there are some other important considerations in choosing a confidant(e). After each of the following statements, write the names of three people in your life who best fit it:

Humility: Understand their own frailty, have gone through their own share of pain with their eyes open, and have experienced coming out of their own emotional bondage to a significant degree

_____   _____   _____

Accepting of others: Accept themselves and others as being subject to human weakness; do not gossip about, criticize, or mock those who admit to having darkness within

_____   _____   _____

Compassion: Empathize with your weaknesses because they recognize that we all have human frailties

_____   _____   _____

CHOOSING MY COMPANION

Nonjudgmental: Accept you and love you even if they do not approve of some things you have done or been involved in

_____   _____   _____

Good listener: Listen and allow you to express honest feelings and confused ideas without condemning you

_____   _____   _____

Consistent: Can be depended on to be fairly stable at a time when you may be unstable

_____   _____   _____

Truthful: Remind you of the truth and act as a balance to point you back toward reality when you are not seeing life clearly

_____   _____   _____

Faithful: Keep your confidences

_____   _____   _____

Nothing to gain: Do not have a personal interest in your image or how quickly you work through your emotional bondage

_____   _____   _____

Encouraging: Can see beyond where you are and who you see yourself to be today, and can point you in the direction of a brighter future

_____   _____   _____

Available: Can and will make themselves available to you to a reasonable degree

_____   _____   _____

THE EMOTIONAL FREEDOM WORKBOOK

Whose names did you write most often? _____

_____

_____

List the names in the order you would prefer as first, second, and third choices for your companion:

1. _____ 2. _____ 3. _____

Contact your first choice and ask him or her to be your companion as you complete this workbook. A workbook companion of the same sex as you is recommended to avoid unhelpful emotional complications or attachments.

Finding a Support Group

We're only as sick as the secrets we keep.—Anonymous

Once you have partnered with someone who will give you strength and encouragement as you complete this workbook, it will be very helpful for you to also establish a support system—a group of people who will keep you alert to your old patterns of thinking and reacting. They will encourage you and build you up as you move toward emotional freedom. Depending on your personal style, you may have difficulty reaching out and trying to assemble a support network. If so, you'll need to rely a little more than usual on the partner you chose. Ask him or her to advise and encourage you as you

- decide what you need from people before you approach them to be a part of your support network. If you know precisely the extent of the commitment you are looking for and the depth of the relationship you are seeking, it will be easier for them to make a decision about whether they can make the commitment. For example, are you looking for a daily or weekly phone call? A monthly one-on-one meeting? A biweekly group meeting?
- talk to several people so you won't be devastated when some decide not to participate. Don't take their decision personally. People are very busy, and sometimes they are dealing with their own shame and

feelings of inadequacy. It is important for you not to take people's "no" answers as rejection!

- make sure your workbook "partner" is both holding your hand and holding you accountable as you establish your support network.

Part 1

Shame

It's kind of hard to explain. . . . I just feel like I'm always "bad." It's sort of like I have a guilty conscience, except I can't quite put my finger on what I've actually done wrong. And when I really do mess up, I'm overwhelmed with humiliation. I want to run and hide where nobody can find me.—Ron M.

Shame is an emotional terrorist. It is the inner pain that comes from accepting the belief that something is inherently wrong with us. It makes us feel "less" than others. It is quite different from feeling guilty for some wrong we have committed. Shame is feeling guilty for the kind of person we believe ourselves to be. Shame is feeling guilty just for being whoever we are.

Shame holds us hostage because when we feel ashamed, we live under a shadow. We are in bondage to the past, imprisoned by our present fears, and unable to face the future unhindered and unafraid. Our activities are constantly accompanied by a nagging sense of guilt, and any problem overwhelms us with feelings of failure and humiliation.

The story of Cinderella is a story of gaining freedom from shame. Cinderella couldn't go to the ball because she wasn't like the other girls in the kingdom. The invitation said that all eligible maidens were to attend. But Cinderella's stepmother and wicked stepsisters made it clear to her that she did not qualify. Cinderella was told that girls like her were not eligible for the good things of life. They pointed out all the evidence: she was just a scullery maid; she was dirty; she didn't have the proper dress; she didn't have refined manners; she had to work and couldn't enjoy the luxury of taking time away for parties. Their ridicule and abuse almost convinced Cinderella to give up hope. She almost conceded. Maybe girls like her weren't eligible for the good things of life. In her moment of shame and disappointment Cinderella threw herself to the ground and sobbed, "Now, I'll never go to the ball."

The turning point in the story came when Cinderella's fairy godmother appeared and rekindled the dream within her heart. Thanks to her fairy godmother's belief in her, Cinderella was able to envision herself as one of the eligible maidens instead of an outcast. The benefits of freedom from shame for Cinderella were much the same as the benefits you will receive when you gain freedom from shame. She was welcome to attend the party. She was able to fit in and feel that she belonged. She was able to acquire the things she needed to go where she wanted to go and do what she wanted to do. She was able to bring out the beauty and grace that were always within her but were covered with the rags of poverty and the ashes in which she lived. She was able to take advantage of the opportunity for new and wonderful relationships. She was able to hold her head high with a sense of self-respect. She was able to have fun, to laugh and dance and sing and, most important, to give and receive love. Ultimately, she was able to escape the abusive home and family life that contributed to keeping her in bondage to shame. She was able to defy the lie that said she was eligible for nothing more than a life locked away as someone's slave.

A turning point in your story will come the moment you are sincerely able to envision what life could become when you are freed from the bondage of

SHAME

shame. Dare to dream of what life could be like if you knew that you were eligible for the good things, that you were not disqualified.

We encourage you to explore the mysteries of your shame and to honestly consider the possibilities offered to you in this workbook. We think you'll soon discover that overcoming shame is an important first step toward emotional freedom.

Healthy and Unhealthy Shame

The lifestyle of good people is like sunlight at dawn that keeps getting brighter until broad daylight.—Proverbs 4:18 CEV

Janice walked into the church, feeling as if everyone was looking at her. Just days before she had been romantically involved with one of the assistant pastors of the church—behind his wife's back. Although she had told herself, *It can't be wrong if it feels so right,* a sense of shame overwhelmed her as she walked into the sanctuary. She wanted to think her feelings were based on the judgmental attitudes of others, but deep inside she knew better: no one else was even aware of her behavior.

Kathleen sat in the PTA meeting longing to speak up, but afraid to open her mouth. She and her three children had talked openly in their home about a major drug abuse problem at the high school campus, and she could tell by listening that the other parents either weren't aware of the problem or didn't want to acknowledge it. But Kathleen was embarrassed by the fact that she was a stay-at-home mom, and that the mothers who were doing all the talking were professional women with college degrees and high-paying jobs. In fact, one was a well-known adolescent psychologist. *They'll never listen to me anyway,* Kathleen told herself. *They'll just think I'm a troublemaker if I tell them what I've heard.*

There are two kinds of shame: healthy shame and unhealthy shame. Unhealthy shame, like Kathleen's, is a painful and overwhelming feeling that drives you away from others and eventually causes you to turn against yourself.

SHAME

Healthy shame, like Janice's, is a personal moral and emotional smoke detector. Just as a smoke detector can forewarn you of the danger of fire that could destroy your home if left to burn unabated, healthy shame signals whenever you are about to enter a potentially dangerous personal situation. As long as you heed the warning given by healthy shame, avoiding behavior and situations that are shameful, you will benefit from your internal security system.

Here is a comparison between healthy shame and unhealthy shame. In each section rate yourself on a scale of 1 to 10 (1 means not descriptive of you at any time; 10 means always descriptive of you).

Healthy Shame   Rating

1. You see your behavior as separate from "who you are." You may do something bad, but you don't take that as evidence that you are essentially a bad person (although you realize that every person is flawed and imperfect).   _____

2. You separate bad experiences from "who you are." Something bad may happen to you or you may be treated abusively, but you don't assume that you deserve such treatment.   _____

3. You see normal lapses, errors, and failures as part of being human. They may act as catalysts, prompting you to make changes toward a more positive direction in life, but they do not overwhelm you.   _____

4. You see avoidance of shame-producing behavior as a way to protect yourself from pain and destruction.   _____

5. You see "breaking the rules"—violation of your boundaries—as a problem that needs to be corrected to reduce the discomfort of the shame you experience.   _____

6. You trust that shame is a temporary feeling of discomfort, which will dissipate when you move away from "breaking the rules."   _____

7. You see your life as valuable, and shame as something built into your being to protect the sanctity of your life. _____

8. You try to live within the boundaries of socially acceptable behavior and take steps to fit in with society. You act in ways that protect your privacy, and you practice discretion in your relationships. _____

Total: _____

Add your ratings. If your total equals

> 39 or under: You need to give more attention to the subject of developing healthy shame. Please complete this part of the workbook, and if you continue to struggle with these issues, call 1-800-NEW-LIFE for further help.

> 40 or over: You're generally healthy, but you may need to work on specific areas where you have difficulties.

Unhealthy Shame   Rating

1. You see wrong behavior or failings as a reflection of "who you are"—your true identity. When you do something bad or make a mistake, you see that as evidence that you are flawed. _____

2. You accept part of the blame when others violate you. You see yourself as someone who deserves to be abused or treated poorly. _____

3. You see normal lapses, errors, and failures as the revelation of your true nature, which is flawed, rather than as a part of being human. You may feel overwhelmed when you experience such a lapse because you think it reveals that something is terribly wrong with you. _____

4. You see avoidance of shame-producing behavior or lifestyle as futile since you believe the behavior or lifestyle is the natural result of being the kind of person you consider yourself to be. _____

5. You regard trying to change your life for the better as living a lie or being hypocritical. You believe your steps in a positive direction are phony, and you negate them instead of viewing them as evidence that you can change. _____

6. Whenever you experience a normal human failing, make an honest mistake, suffer a disappointment, violate your moral standards, or have your boundaries violated by others, it may trigger a downward spiral of depression or addictive behavior. _____

7. You may appear to others to be utterly shameless in some or all areas of your life. When you shut down the influence of healthy shame, you lose the strength of your boundaries. You may eventually be worn down to the point that you give in to your overwhelming shame and act out in ways that show no sense of healthy shame and no awareness of legitimate moral guilt. _____

Total: _____

Add your ratings. If your total equals

35 or over: You are dealing with a significant degree of unhealthy shame.

34 or under: You are probably generally healthy. Everyone experiences shame to some degree, so if your score is 34 or under, your shame is probably manageable.

Write a description of how healthy shame operates in your life at this time. Also note any specific experiences that might have violated your healthy shame throughout your life, causing a breakdown of your barriers or a shutoff of the influence of healthy shame. _____

_____

_____

Write a description of how unhealthy shame operates in your life at this time. Note specific areas where you feel inferior to others because of a sense of shame that makes you fear something is wrong with you._____

_____

_____

Identifying the
Symptoms of Shame

In the depth of winter, I finally learned that within me lay an invincible summer.—Albert Camus

Unhealthy shame is an internal matter. People may look at you and never dream that your life is limited by shameful feelings. You may seem to be far different from the way you see yourself since shame causes you to cover up the real you. There are specific symptoms of unhealthy shame. Check the following symptoms that are evident in your life. Put a star beside the ones that are most typical of you.

___ 1. You simply can't bring yourself to do things, go places, or be around people because you feel intimidated.

___ 2. You experience recurrent bouts of depression.

___ 3. You are in self-isolation: physically or emotionally distancing yourself from others, particularly those you care about most.

___ 4. You pretend to be other than you are.

___ 5. You rely on habits or substances to medicate inner pain and self-loathing.

___ 6. You exaggerate and/or lie about yourself, your accomplishments, and your lifestyle; you brag and name-drop.

___ 7. Your public identity and your private self are markedly different.

___ 8. You have had suicidal thoughts.*

THE EMOTIONAL FREEDOM WORKBOOK

__ 9. You assume the blame when someone treats you poorly or hurts you.

__ 10. You make excuses for people who abuse you or treat you with disrespect.

__ 11. You are unable to accept yourself as only human; instead, you see yourself as subhuman or superhuman. You are unable to accept both the good and the bad within you; rather, you cling to a view of yourself that is all bad or all good, or you alternate between the two.

__ 12. You keep secrets about yourself, and you feel bound to carry them with you to the grave.

__ 13. You keep a shameful part of your life separate from the rest of your life, even in your own mind, so that your behavior in one area is markedly different from the rest of your life (this split-off part may violate your values and eventually threaten your well-being).

__ 14. You deny the nature and severity of your addictions.

__ 15. You lose yourself in the needs of others: busying yourself taking care of others; rescuing; trying to control, fix, or change them; and trying to solve their problems while neglecting your life.

__ 16. You feel driven to achieve, overachieve, and excel to feel okay about yourself; you try to prove your worth by what you do.

__ 17. You focus on the flaws and failings of others; being judgmental and critical draws attention away from you or consoles you that you aren't as bad as the object of your criticism.

__ 18. You defy societal norms—dressing, acting, and relating in ways that are socially unacceptable. If you defy the rules of society, you can console yourself that any rejection is the rejection of your appearance or manners, and you can distance yourself from personal rejection.

__ 19. You associate primarily with people on an extreme end of the social ladder. (Some people associate with those they view as losers because that is the only group they feel they belong with and can be accepted by. Others associate only with people of status because they derive their sense of self-worth from being accepted by those they believe to be above them.)

SHAME

__ 20. You break off relationships with people you care about deeply before they have a chance to know the real you and reject you.

__ 21. You fear expressing your honest opinions and feelings; you adapt your opinions to try to match those expressed by people you are associating with at the time.

__ 22. You are lonely.

__ 23. You fear being found out as a phony.

__ 24. You are a perfectionist, trying to make up for who you are by doing everything perfectly.

__ 25. You fear failure, which keeps you from trying new ventures.

__ 26. You are unable to ask for help because you feel that admitting need exposes your area of inadequacy.

__ 27. You resist setting personal goals in the areas where you have a sense of shame.

Review the items you checked as symptoms of shame in your life. Write the three that are most prevalent. Describe specific incidents where these three symptoms of shame were manifested recently.

1. _____

2. _____

3. _____

Write your thoughts about your symptoms of shame. How do you feel when you see the effects of shame on your life? _____

_____

_____

*If you are experiencing any sort of suicidal thoughts, do not continue to work on this book. Set it aside for now and talk to your pastor or therapist, or call 1-800-NEW-LIFE.

Shame and Addictions

You will not die from sobriety.—Anonymous

Shame and addictions feed on each other. You cannot gain freedom from shame while you are actively medicating the pain of life by relying on addictive-compulsive behavior. You must deal with both issues at the same time.

The addictive process involves using a mood-altering substance or experience to temporarily escape the pain of life. And it isn't always a major, life-threatening addiction to substances such as drugs or alcohol. It can be far more subtle—sometimes even a good thing carried to the extreme.

Whatever the substance or experience, you feel better for a while when you give in to your addictions. But once the emotional high dissipates, you need progressively more of whatever you use to get the previous level of relief. Eventually, you violate previously held boundaries. What was once considered taboo or off-limits becomes something you allow, even though you offend your conscience. You then have to deal with guilt, self-condemnation, and the consequences of your behavior while "under the influence." When you once again face yourself and the consequences of your behavior, there is more fuel for the fire of shame already burning within you. Your aggravated feelings of shame cause tremendous pain. You are drawn back to the addictive substance or experience in hopes of deadening the pain that feels overwhelming.

SHAME

What do you do to temporarily alter your mood when you are feeling pain associated with your unhealthy shame?_____

_____

_____

_____

_____

What substances or experiences do you use to "feel better"? _____

_____

_____

_____

_____

Place a check next to any of the following that you have used in an addictive or an obsessive way. Circle the ones you are using now (or have used within the past six months).

    __ Alcohol
    __ Other people's problems
    __ Gambling
    __ Overeating
    __ Shopping/spending money
    __ Drugs
    __ Relationship/romance
    __ Religious addiction
    __ Sex addiction (including pornography)
    __ Workaholism
    __ Other: _____

Counselors have learned to recognize something called a *cycle of addiction*. Here's how it looks:

CYCLE OF ADDICTION

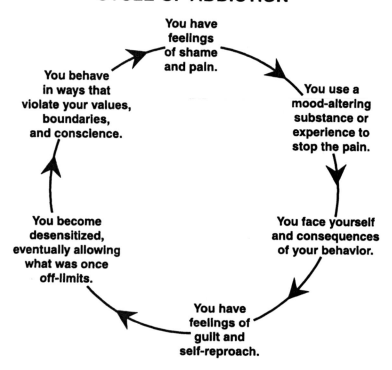

Shame will drag you back into addictive-compulsive behavior, and addictive-compulsive behavior will drag you back into shame. This vicious cycle must be stopped at the point of the addiction while also dealing with the underlying issues of shame.

How do you see addiction and shame interrelating in your life?

_____

_____

What do you think you can do to break the cycle of shame and addictive-compulsive behavior? _____

_____

_____

SHAME

Living without your addiction does not have to mean ongoing pain for you. By dealing with shame-related issues at the same time you seek treatment for addiction, you have the best chance possible of finding emotional freedom. You can find a way toward a truly happy life without the desperate need to medicate yourself to enjoy living.

Here are some suggestions:

- Tell someone that you may have an addiction.
- Call a treatment program and get involved.
- Attend a support group or a twelve-step recovery group.
- Make an appointment with a counselor who specializes in helping persons with your particular addiction.

Setting Goals for Getting Rid of Shame

A goal properly set is a goal partially reached.—Zig Ziglar

Setting goals sounds like a huge challenge for a person in bondage to shame. Shame tells you there is no use trying to reach a goal because you will only fail—again. Shame warns you that having a clearly defined goal will clearly prove your deficiency. If you deeply believe or fear that there is something inherently wrong with you, you will resist setting specific goals that could be used to measure your worth.

Here's what we mean by *goal:* "a clearly defined statement of your desires and dreams set in measured terms and pursued within a specific time frame."

Are you afraid to set goals? That is one indicator that shame has you bound in a particular area of life. Usually, you'll feel more comfortable setting goals in areas where shame is not a factor since you believe you have a chance to reach them. Even if you don't reach them, you won't interpret that to mean something is deeply wrong with you. The challenge, then, is to learn to set and reach goals in the areas where unhealthy shame has you in bondage. This is very important to your process of overcoming unhealthy shame.

Let's try to determine where shame is limiting you most. Chances are, the areas where you have no goals and have no desire to set any are the areas most inhibited by shame.

First, we will divide your life into these key areas:

- Family
- Career
- Spiritual
- Financial
- Physical
- Mental/intellectual
- Social

Now, ask yourself the following three questions about each of these areas of life. Circle Y (=Yes) or N (=No):

1. Do I know what I desire and dream? Family Y/N, Career Y/N, Spiritual Y/N, Financial Y/N, Physical Y/N, Intellectual, Y/N, Social Y/N

2. Have I clarified my desires and dreams into specific measurable terms—what, when, where, and how—so I can know when I have reached my goal? Family Y/N, Career Y/N, Spiritual Y/N, Financial Y/N, Physical Y/N, Intellectual, Y/N, Social Y/N

3. Am I pursuing my goals within a specified time frame? Family Y/N, Career Y/N, Spiritual Y/N, Financial Y/N, Physical Y/N, Intellectual, Y/N, Social Y/N

In what areas are you *not* inhibited by shame? How do you feel about yourself in these areas? What difference can you see in your view of yourself in shame-affected areas and areas unaffected by shame?

Reducing shame is a legitimate goal in and of itself. But since shame is an obstacle to setting and reaching other goals, it has to be considered as a factor in your efforts to set other goals. Complete the following sentences:

Shame keeps me from _____.

Shame causes me to feel uncomfortable whenever I _____
_____.

Shame keeps me from going _____.

Shame keeps me from having a relationship with _____.

Shame keeps me from being _____.

Now complete these sentences:

I want to overcome shame in the _____ area of my life so I can experience
the freedom to _____.

I want to feel more comfortable when I _____.

I want to try _____.

I want to develop a relationship with _____.

I want to become _____.

From what you have written with regard to setting goals, what is one short-term
goal you can reach by the end of thirty days? _____
_____

What is a more challenging goal that you can try to reach within a year?
_____
_____

Clearing Away Legitimate Guilt

If we say that we have no sin, we deceive ourselves, and the truth is not in us. If we confess our sins, He is faithful and just to forgive us our sins and to cleanse us from all unrighteousness.—*1 John 1:8–9* NKJV

- Are guilt and shame clearly distinguished in your life?
- Do you believe there is no forgiveness for people like you?
- How has shame cut you off from the forgiveness offered by God?
- How do you deal with guilt feelings?

With guilt, you are troubled by what you have done. With shame, you are troubled by who you are. Guilt and shame are closely related, often becoming a confused jumble of painful emotions. When guilt and shame become intertwined, the accumulation of pain, the desire to escape yourself, and the weight of your burdens can threaten to overwhelm you. By identifying and resolving legitimate guilt, you get your shame more clearly into focus so that you can begin to deal with it appropriately.

Guilt and shame are similar in that both can cause you to want to hide, distance yourself from God and others, and try to make amends to feel better. Both can evoke deep feelings of sadness, fear, self-loathing, and remorse. The difference between legitimate guilt and shame is that guilt is related to behavior and shame is related to your being.

True guilt is experienced when you do something that is wrong or fail to do what you know to be right. Legitimate guilt also occurs when you break a commitment that you entered into willingly. The solution for legitimate guilt is to accept responsibility for having violated moral boundaries, confess the exact nature of your wrongs to God, yourself, and another human being, and seek forgiveness. You also reduce your burden of guilt when you identify persons who have been harmed by your wrongs and make amends to them, except when to do so would injure them or others.

Healthy shame may evoke feelings of sadness and disappointment when you realize there are limitations to what you can do and be for others, but these feelings do not overwhelm you.

Unhealthy shame causes you to condemn yourself on the basis of who you are and the limitations within your life. You feel overwhelmed with sadness and self-hatred whenever you realize that you are less than the person you wish you were.

You may try to rid yourself of guilt by throwing out all the rules and choosing to deny your allegiance to previously held moral standards. Deciding to ignore the rules doesn't eliminate guilt. It increases guilt.

To deal with unhealthy shame, you must get rid of legitimate guilt in your life. And you have to be able to determine which is which.

On the scale following each statement, the far left side is the extreme guilt pole.

On the far right is the extreme unhealthy shame pole.

Read each statement, honestly reflect on your response, then mark a point on the scale between the two extremes that indicates where your reaction falls between the two poles. Remember, guilt has to do with what you've done; shame has to do with who you are.

I feel inadequate.

GUILT <———————————————> SHAME

I want to hide and avoid people.

GUILT <———————————————> SHAME

SHAME

I feel like distancing myself from God.

GUILT <————————————> SHAME

I feel like making amends for my failures.

GUILT <————————————> SHAME

I feel sad.

GUILT <————————————> SHAME

I feel fearful.

GUILT <————————————> SHAME

I feel self-loathing.

GUILT <————————————> SHAME

I feel sorry and regretful.

GUILT <————————————> SHAME

After you have considered your reactions, write down the actions that have caused you to feel guilt. What have you done that was wrong, inappropriate, or a violation of established boundaries? _____

_____

_____

In your own words, write about how the following Scriptures apply to you, the things you have done (or left undone), and your feelings of guilt:

"There is therefore now no condemnation to those who are in Christ Jesus" (Rom. 8:1 NKJV). _____

_____

_____

"If we confess our sins, He is faithful and just to forgive us our sins and to cleanse us from all unrighteousness" (1 John 1:9 NKJV)._____

_____

_____

"In this the love of God was manifested toward us, that God has sent His only begotten Son into the world, that we might live through Him. In this is love, not that we loved God, but that He loved us and sent His Son to be the propitiation for our sins" (1 John 4:9–10 NKJV). _____

_____

_____

These Scriptures, and the truth they communicate, are specifically intended to remove guilt from the life of the Christian. Here are some steps you can take for living your life without guilt:

Step One: Whenever you experience guilty feelings, stop to examine their source.

Step Two: Identify behaviors causing you legitimate guilt.

Step Three: Acknowledge (confess) the exact nature of your wrongs to God, yourself, and another human being.

Step Four: Determine that you will change your behavior and seek God's help in doing so.

Step Five: Accept the forgiveness offered by God.

Step Six: Seek out someone who understands the grace and love of God to help you learn to accept God's forgiveness.

Finding Your Sources
of Shame

"My grace is sufficient for you, for power is perfected in weakness." Most gladly, therefore, I will rather boast about my weaknesses, that the power of Christ may dwell in me. Therefore I am well content with weaknesses, with insults, with distresses, with persecutions, with difficulties, for Christ's sake; for when I am weak, then I am strong.—2 Corinthians 12:9–10 NASB

Once you have come to terms with the guilt that has troubled you, you can begin to deal with feelings of shame. There are three possible reasons for your feelings of unhealthy shame. You may feel

1. shame placed on you by others.
2. shame derived from continuous exposure to a shameful environment.
3. shame resulting from one isolated incident.

Shame placed on you by others means that you've been told or taught that there is something inherently wrong with you. It may have come at a time when your identity was still being formed in childhood or adolescence. And if the condemnation came from someone close to you, someone important in your life, or someone to whom you had revealed yourself, it had greater power to influence your present view of yourself.

THE EMOTIONAL FREEDOM WORKBOOK

Take a moment and think of an example for each of the following statements. Some of them may not apply to you. If so, write N/A in the space. If there are too many examples for some of the other statements, continue your answers on a separate sheet of paper.

I feel ashamed because of something I was taught about myself at an early age.

_____

_____

I feel ashamed because of verbal abuse. I was called names that defined my worth in negative terms, such as stupid, idiot, good-for-nothing, or ugly, or I was told I would never amount to anything._____

_____

I feel ashamed because I was identified as the scapegoat of my family, the troublemaker, the black sheep, the outcast. _____

_____

I feel ashamed because I was teased by other children, and I was told I deserved to be picked on because something was wrong with me or my family.

_____

_____

I feel ashamed because shame was used to bring me into submission.

_____

I feel ashamed because of nonverbal cues I received. I was discriminated against because of my race, sex, color, physical appearance, religious beliefs, level of wealth, or poverty._____

_____

SHAME

I feel ashamed because I was punished for my individuality.

_____

_____

Shame that happened because of a shameful environment would involve living in ongoing circumstances that degrade your human dignity or situations that make you feel abnormal or inferior to your peers. If they apply, write examples of the following statements. If they do not apply, write N/A. If your answer is too long for the lines, complete it on a separate sheet of paper.

I feel ashamed because of parental neglect—my basic needs were not met.

_____

_____

I feel ashamed because there was socially unacceptable behavior within my family that was known within the community. _____

_____

_____

I feel ashamed because I lived (live) within a family where alcohol, drugs, or other addictions or compulsions caused life to be out of control and unpredictable; where personal boundaries were often violated. _____

_____

_____

I feel ashamed because I lived (live) with ongoing sexual and/or physical abuse.

_____

_____

I feel ashamed because of growing up in a "perfect" family where there was (is) constant criticism for any failure to meet the expected standards.

_____

THE EMOTIONAL FREEDOM WORKBOOK

I feel ashamed because I grew up (presently live) in poverty, in filthy conditions, with socially unacceptable clothing. _____

_____

I feel ashamed because of physical abnormalities. _____

_____

An isolated experience can "brand" you with shame. A particular incident may overshadow you for the rest of your life, leaving you feeling indelibly marked in a negative way. Write examples from your life that fit the following statements. If they don't apply, write N/A; use a separate sheet of paper for lengthy answers.

I feel ashamed because I violated my moral standards in a way that was shocking to me. _____

_____

I feel ashamed because I was publicly exposed in an area where I have done wrong or feel vulnerable. _____

_____

I feel ashamed because I was forced to violate my sexual boundaries through rape or some other violent sexual assault. _____

_____

I feel ashamed because of public humiliation or rejection. _____

_____

I feel ashamed because of rejection and/or abandonment by someone to whom I have revealed my inner self. _____

_____

SHAME

I feel ashamed because of suicide by someone close to me. _____
_____

I feel ashamed because I lost my job (this is particularly significant if you were fired because of something you cannot change, such as being too old, or because of not being able to handle the work or some failure to perform adequately).
_____
_____

I feel ashamed because of a terrible event that occurred when I was very young, such as the death of a loved one, a divorce, or a severe physical injury or disability. _____
_____

In the spaces below, under each heading, write the sources of shame in your life.

Others	Environment	Single Incident
_____	_____	_____
_____	_____	_____

Once you identify the sources of your shame, you will be able to identify resources to help you deal with each one, finding healing for the brokenness and a new perspective for the future. God wants you to be set free from the emotional bondage that shame creates, and he makes his power available to you in the midst of your weakness.

That's What Friends Are For

There is nothing so moving—not even acts of love or hate—as to discover that one is not alone.—Robert Ardrey

Casey fell and injured her head. The experience was terribly frightening. In the hospital emergency room she was snatched from the arms of her mother. Under glaring lights, a man in a mask held her face. Another man plunged a large hypodermic needle into her forehead, then he took a needle and thread, sticking the needle into her flesh time and again. She heard them say they were giving her stitches.

Two years later, Casey visited her mother immediately following the birth of another child. At the family birthing center siblings were welcome to attend the birth. However, the nurse asked her to leave so she could give the mother stitches. Casey was horrified. She decided she had to do something to make sure she never again had to get stitches.

For the next few months Casey refused to eat meat. Her parents were concerned, but they didn't confront the issue. Finally, she said to her mother, "Mommy, I really would like to eat meat again, but I just can't! You told me that I need to eat meat so I can grow up to be strong and healthy. And if I grow up, I will have a baby. And if I have a baby, they will give me stitches again. And I made up my mind, I am going to make sure no one ever gives me stitches again!"

In her sincere attempt at self-protection Casey had given up something she enjoyed. She sacrificed a part of her life on the altar of an erroneous belief. Maybe you have done something like this. In hopes of protecting yourself, you may still be living by beliefs that needlessly deprive you of intimacy, trust, a church home, friendships, good feelings, rest, peace of mind, and the like. You may seek to control, manipulate, rescue, and fix others in the belief that you will ensure your security. The tragedy is that controlling others is not possible, and it holds no power to ensure security. Life is not, nor will it ever be, completely within your control. You can know greater hope of security by reevaluating beliefs foundational to your codependent behavior and challenging them.

Once you've identified the sources of your unhealthy shame, you can actively discover and gain access to resources and support to reduce the power that shame has over you. Here are some very important resources:

- You—your intellect, energy, determination, courage, and hope for the future—are your primary resource.
- New skills change the way you live and think.
- Knowledge gives you a new perspective.
- Individuals lend support to your efforts.
- Groups help you eliminate your shame.
- God is committed to your emotional freedom so that you can become all he intends you to become.

Here are the steps to finding resources in any area of interest. Since your needs are unique, you will need to follow these steps to find specific resources for you:

Step One: Identify the area where you need help or more information.

Step Two: Check at your local library for books on the topic or related topics. If necessary, ask a librarian to recommend some books on the topic or guide you to the section of the library that holds the books you need.

Step Three: Contact organizations that are set up to deal with issues related to your area of interest. Use the telephone directory to find churches, agencies, recovery groups and, if appropriate, treatment centers or counselors.

A growing network of treatment centers and recovery groups has resources available. You can contact counseling offices, treatment centers, or universities and usually get leads about people, groups, and organizations that help individuals in specific ways. If you are a Christian believer, you will want to find a Bible-based program. Please call 1-800-NEW-LIFE for further information.

You can call the offices of radio talk shows that deal with issues related to your area of interest. Radio talk programs keep an extensive listing of guests who address various topics. They will probably have a list of referrals to groups and organizations as well.

The best resources are human resources. Within your community, there are church groups, men's/women's groups, recovery groups, parenting groups, educational seminars, and so on. You can find these resources through your local chamber of commerce.

The real key to finding information and resources is to keep on seeking, keep on asking, and keep on knocking on doors. Once you know what you want to accomplish, what tasks you need to complete to reach your goals, and what information or help you lack, it's just a matter of persistent effort to track down the resources.

You are not alone. We hope that you have established a network of supportive friends and family members who are willing to help you. Call them when you need them—don't allow yourself to be isolated. God can use them to help you find resources!

What are three things you can do today to begin tracking down the resources you need to deal with your shame?

1. _____

2. _____

3. _____

SHAME

Do these three things! Ask your support person to keep you accountable.

As you prepare yourself to open up to others, you may experience feelings of vulnerability, and you may struggle with a strong desire to run away from the very people you hope to trust. Sometimes this reaction is the by-product of your unhealthy shame. But it may also be evidence of unrevealed parts of yourself. It's important for you to explore some of the hidden places in your heart.

After reflecting upon them, write honest answers to the following questions:

Do I have secrets that I have never told anyone? What are they?

_____

_____

Do I fear that if others know my secrets, they will reject me and/or humiliate me? (Describe your worst fear regarding this possibility, then write out why it might be wise to take the risk of revealing your secrets.) _____

_____

_____

Don't feel troubled if you aren't ready to reveal your secrets to someone yet. That's okay. As you prepare yourself to do so, let your support person and your support group know that you are working through some concerns. Talk to them about your fears.

While you are preparing yourself to entrust your secrets to the people you've asked to support you, consider the other side of the coin: Whom can you *not* trust? Although no other person is able to deem you an acceptable human being, there are sometimes those who persist in treating you shamefully. This can be the case whether you share your secrets with them or not. Clearly, "friends" who shame you when you aren't revealing your inner thoughts are going to shame you even more when you do!

You can learn to limit the influence of people in your life who shame you. People around you may continue to spew out potentially shame-producing words, attitudes, and behavior, but you can learn to stop the influence before it reaches your heart.

List the people who cause you to feel unhealthy shame through words, attitudes, or behavior: _____

_____

_____

Consider these ways to limit the influence of shame-producing people in your life:

- You can limit your exposure to them.
- You can counterbalance the shame others try to place on you by getting a different perspective from those who are supportive and positive about you.
- You can refuse to be manipulated by objectively determining that you have not done anything wrong. Refuse to respond to the condemnation. Instead calmly, but firmly, explain that you don't accept their estimation of you.
- You can take time out. Emotionally step back from the situation— consider what their behavior and attitude mean about them, not just what they mean about you.

In which relationships would limiting your exposure to the other person be a good way to limit the shameful influences in your life? _____

_____

_____

_____

SHAME

Whom can you call on to counterbalance the condemnation and shame others try to place on you? _____

_____

_____

Take a moment to think about the people in your life who shame you. Journal your thoughts about what their behavior says about their insecurities, problems, hurts, or fears that may have nothing to do with you. _____

_____

_____

Recall a situation where someone did something that you allowed to produce shame within you. Now imagine three or four different ways that you could have responded to limit the shame you accepted. Apply the advice given here to imagine positive ways to deal with potentially shame-producing situations. Write your thoughts about the possibilities._____

_____

_____

Drawing Close to Those Who Lessen Your Shame

A friend loves at all times, and a brother is born for adversity.
—Proverbs 17:17 NKJV

As a child, Karen went without shoes most of the time. When school was in session, she was often ashamed of the hand-me-down shoes her parents made her wear. Many times she hid her feet under the desk in hopes the other children wouldn't notice how outdated and marred her shoes were. Sometimes she succeeded. Other times her peers delighted themselves by teasing her about her shoes. Karen never told anyone what happened. It seemed ridiculous, especially because such a little thing was a powerful source of shame for her.

Karen had forgotten all about it until a moment came when the shame of her childhood was rekindled. Both Karen and her husband lost their jobs suddenly and unexpectedly when she was five months pregnant. She decided not to try to find a new job until after the baby came. Her husband was unable to find employment for several months, although he sought work diligently. Eventually, their finances dwindled to almost nothing, the baby was nearly due, and Karen was sinking into depression.

The night before Easter, Karen was trying to find something decent to wear

SHAME

to church but wasn't having much luck because her body and feet had swollen out of proportion to her clothes and shoes. The only nice dress that fit had a stain on it, and the only shoes she could squeeze her feet into were badly worn. Karen's friend Sue was visiting that evening. When Karen came out of the bedroom to see if her outfit was passable, she was in no mood to handle criticism. Not realizing how badly Karen was feeling about herself, her husband blurted out, "You can't wear those shoes. They look awful." Karen burst into tears. The pain of her childhood shame came rushing in on her. She relived the feelings of shame she had known when, as a child, she'd tried to hide her feet under the school desk so no one would notice the symbol of her poverty.

After a few moments, Karen gained her composure. Sue asked if she would mind coming with her on some errands and Karen agreed. The first stop Sue made was at a shoe store where she sat her friend down and helped her select a pair of new shoes that fit. At church the next day Karen didn't have to hide her feet because she had a friend who knew how to lessen her shame without making her feel like a charity case.

A person who lessens your shame is someone who

- sees beyond the circumstances and garb of the moment to the beauty within you.
- understands the pain and humiliation associated with your shame and takes action to relieve the pain and protect you from humiliation.
- is in a position to help you cover or replace some of the things that symbolize your shame, the things that cause you to lower your head, fear exposure, and feel ashamed of yourself.
- loves you enough to help you see yourself in a new light.

Write an example of someone in your life who helped cover your shame:

_____

_____

THE EMOTIONAL FREEDOM WORKBOOK

Make a conscious decision to draw near the people you believe have the love and respect for you that will help you overcome your shame. Call one or more of these people and make arrangements to spend some time together next week. If you can recall specific incidents where others' kindness and respect for you helped you feel better about yourself, call them or drop them a note to say, "Thank you!"

Know the Real God

Do not fear, for you will not be ashamed;
Neither be disgraced, for you will not be put to shame;
For you will forget the shame of your youth.—Isaiah 54:4 NKJV

Negative religion—which plays on your sense of shame in order to manipulate you into submission—is very damaging. When you already feel that you are terribly flawed, being scolded or harangued in the name of God does nothing to draw you nearer to God or to help you escape your torment. In fact, just the opposite is true—negative religion plays a role in keeping you in bondage to shame.

Shame is the opposite of what God desires for you. From beginning to end, Scripture reveals God's plan to free you from the bondage of shame. In the opening chapters of the Bible, man and woman are naked and unashamed. With the fall of humankind, shame enters the world, and God goes to work devising a plan to cover the nakedness. He knows this is essential because shame keeps people in hiding from themselves, others, and God. The prophet Isaiah proclaimed the desire of God's heart when he said,

Instead of your shame you shall have double honor,
And instead of confusion they shall rejoice in their portion.
Therefore in their land they shall possess double;
Everlasting joy shall be theirs. (Isa. 61:7 NKJV)

Write that statement in your own words. _____

_____

What does it tell you about God's desire for his people? _____

_____

When Jesus came to earth as a child, God identified with your shame. Jesus was born under the shadow of reproach because his mother was not married when she became pregnant. As a man, he was continually reprimanded by religious leaders because he associated with a shameful assortment of characters, most notably prostitutes and societal outcasts.

When Jesus died on the cross, he took upon himself the sins and the shame of the whole world. He was mocked, hated, spat upon, stripped naked before the gawking eyes of a jeering mob, ridiculed, rejected, tormented, and left to die because of who he was, not because of something he had done.

The writer to the Hebrews said that Jesus "endured the cross, despising the shame" (12:2 NKJV). He died in humiliation and nakedness so that he could purchase robes of righteousness to cover your shame when you stand before God the Father. The apostle John told believers to "abide in Him, that when He appears, we may have confidence and not be ashamed before Him at His coming" (1 John 2:28 NKJV).

Write what this passage in 1 John means to you today. _____

_____

God offers to cover your shame, and he provides a remedy for the shame at the core of your being. It is a terrible tragedy when people who represent God communicate the message in a way that exposes your shame instead of covering it.

Have you experienced rejection from people who represent God? Briefly describe the situation. _____

_____

_____

Your unhealthy shame may be clouding your interpretation of what is being said and done in the name of God. Write your thoughts about drawing close to God.

_____

_____

Does what you have written actually describe God, or does it describe negative religion? Explain. _____

_____

_____

If you don't know God,

- ask God to reveal himself to you.
- get involved in a Bible study to learn what he is really like.
- continue to seek God. Look for a community of believers who understand and communicate God's grace and unconditional love.
- find a place where God's mercy is celebrated, where the joy of worship comes from understanding God's everlasting love that cannot be vanquished by our humanity.

Here are the elements of a healthy, nonshaming religion:

- Right and wrong are clearly upheld but always in the context of God's unconditional love and willingness to forgive you and cleanse you from all sin.
- When sin is acknowledged, confessed to God, and turned from, it is covered rather than publicly exposed.
- Your standing with God is based on God's grace (unearned favor), not on your performance.
- All people are accepted equally without regard to their outward appearance, worldly status, or wealth.

Take a moment to think about your experiences with religion, churches, and God. How has negative religion exposed or aggravated your sense of shame?

_____

_____

Have you ever entered into a relationship with God by trusting Christ's death on the cross to cover your sins? If so, what has doing this meant to you?

_____

_____

Write your thoughts about Jesus as someone who understands your shame, identifies with you in your shame, and wants to cover your shame.

_____

_____

Is your avoidance of negative religion keeping you from a positive relationship with God? Explain._____

_____

What steps can you take to find a community of people who communicate God's love and grace in a way that helps you find freedom from shame?

_____

_____

Ask God to help you find your way beyond any shame associated with negative religion so that you can receive his guidance in gaining freedom from shame. Then ask yourself these questions:

- If God is willing to cover my spiritual nakedness so that I can stand before him unashamed, am I willing to receive the covering he offers me through Jesus Christ?
- If I were to stand before him now, do I think I would be covered?

Making Changes

You can change the way you see yourself, and in doing so, you will be free to change your life.—Stephen Arterburn

Research has shown that your mind will cling to foundational beliefs and throw out any new ideas that disagree with your preconceived ideas. This is true, even if your beliefs are not based on truth. For example, if you see yourself as ugly and someone offers you a compliment about your appearance, you will automatically dismiss the possibility that the compliment is genuine. Instead you wonder what he wants from you or why he is teasing you. You may wonder what is wrong with him that he can't see how ugly you are.

To change your mind you must take five important steps:

Step One: You must acknowledge your foundational beliefs about yourself and your negative prophecies about your life. One of the ways to determine these beliefs and prophecies is to listen to your self-talk. What do you tell yourself?

Negative beliefs sound like this:

- "I am a loser."
- "I am nothing but trouble."
- "I am stupid."
- "I am a misfit."
- "I am a burden to my loved ones."

Negative prophecies sound like this:

THE EMOTIONAL FREEDOM WORKBOOK

- "I'll never make anything of myself."
- "I'll never have a respectable career."
- "I'll never be able to provide for my family."
- "I'll never marry again because it would be a disaster."
- "I'll never reach my normal weight."

Write down three negative beliefs you hold about yourself.

1. _____
2. _____
3. _____

Write down three negative prophecies you believe about yourself.

1. _____
2. _____
3. _____

Step Two: Challenge your beliefs. Accept the possibility that you may be wrong in your self-condemnation.

Write three reasons that each of your negative beliefs you listed may be wrong. If you find this difficult to do, ask your workbook partner for help.

Negative belief #1:

1. _____
2. _____
3. _____

Negative belief #2:

1. _____
2. _____
3. _____

Negative belief #3:

1. _____
2. _____
3. _____

Write three reasons that each of your negative prophecies you listed may be wrong. Again, if you find this difficult to do, ask for help from your workbook partner.

Negative prophecy #1:

1. _____
2. _____
3. _____

Negative prophecy #2:

1. _____
2. _____
3. _____

Negative prophecy #3:

1. _____
2. _____
3. _____

Step Three: Introduce new evidence that may help you arrive at a new set of beliefs. Accumulate facts that do not fit with your shameful image of yourself. Notice your good qualities that you have previously discounted. Notice what others say they appreciate about you that you have refused to accept.

I have learned that I am _____

_____
_____
_____.

Step Four: Learn to reinterpret the current and historical facts of your life in a new way. Introduce a new theory about your life and yourself that leaves room for the belief that you may be capable, worthwhile, valuable, and acceptable.

I'm beginning to see that I _____

_____

_____

_____.

Step Five: Change the way you talk to yourself and about yourself in your mind. Don't insult yourself.

List the names you call yourself:

I am a _____.

I am a _____.

Erase or scratch out each of the negative words and replace it with a positive word that you can believe in.

I am a _____.

I am a _____.

When you hear yourself saying insulting things to yourself, stop yourself. Replace your negative statement with a positive one. Treat yourself with the same kindness and courtesy you would extend to a person you respect or admire.

Finding a New Audience

You may be much harder on yourself in your own mind than others are in real life. You can learn to see yourself in a more positive light.
—Stephen Arterburn

Jim, a dedicated high school football coach, was acutely aware that his young team consistently lost every game they played away from their home stadium. When they played before a supportive audience of friends and family, they played well, maintained a positive attitude in spite of temporary setbacks, and invariably won the game. When they played before a crowd cheering for the other team, they became self-conscious, focusing on what they did wrong, fearing the humiliation they would experience if they lost, anticipating what might go wrong. The predictable reaction of an unfriendly crowd caused them to hesitate and lose the game.

Jim recognized the pattern and devised a solution that allowed his players to begin winning their out-of-town games. He videotaped every game and reviewed the tape with the team. During the review, he pointed out everything the players did that was right as individuals and as a team. He made corrections as necessary, but the primary focus was on affirming and accentuating the positive. Once the players began to anticipate the postgame reviews, they were playing for their coach and for themselves. When the team learned to play for the new audience, their performance at away games improved dramatically and became more consistent.

When you have an unhealthy sense of shame, you carry an imaginary audience with you. In your mind, people around you are looking down on you, expecting poor performance, and waiting for the opportunity to humiliate you. You feel self-conscious about your flaws. If you see yourself as a loser in the game of life, you dread the mistakes you are sure you will make. And if and when you do stumble or make an error, you are sure that people are watching and demeaning you as a result. Imagining this type of negative audience is a common experience for most adolescents.

People with unhealthy shame often don't move beyond the juvenile struggle to establish a positive personal identity. Shame is often related to symptoms of arrested development and immature behavior. As long as you continue to play to a negative audience that you imagine to be watching your every move and waiting to pounce on any flaw, you will be unable to consistently do your best and win at the game of life.

Consider these questions, and answer them as honestly as possible:

Do you carry around a negative or positive imaginary audience?

_____

_____

_____

How does this audience affect your performance in life? _____

_____

_____

_____

What can you do to limit or get rid of the real negative audience that may be a source of ongoing criticism and shame? _____

_____

_____

— 59 —
SHAME

What can you do to find a place where you are playing before a supportive audience? _____
_____
_____

Are you willing to believe that God is watching you with positive regard and high hopes for your success? _____
_____

How would your life be different if you could really believe this?
_____
_____

Write your thoughts about your audience, whether they cheer or boo your efforts. _____
_____
_____

Write one thing you can do today to limit your exposure to a negative audience.
_____
_____
_____

Take a moment right now to ask God to help you see him on your side, applauding your efforts.

Look for Seeds of Potential

It is never too late to be what you might have been.—George Eliot

Everyone has seeds of potential greatness. To produce fruit, you must plant the seed, nourish it, allow time for it to grow, and protect and tend to the plant until you see the fruit mature. If the seeds are not recognized for what they are and are therefore never planted, nourished, allowed time to grow, and protected and tended during the growth process, they will never produce the fruit they were created to produce.

Shame tells you there are no seeds of greatness within you—only dirt! And if you believe this about yourself, you will not take the necessary steps to grow seeds of greatness into the mature fruit of accomplishment. If you somehow missed the concept that you have to grow and develop the seeds within you before you taste the good fruit in life, you might have given up before you ever had a chance to see the good within you grow to fruition.

Describe the seeds of potential you have taken the time, effort, and energy to nourish and tend. _____

_____

Describe your good qualities—things such as honesty, friendliness, kindness, and trustworthiness. _____

_____

SHAME

Describe how shame has inhibited you from taking action that would develop your seeds of greatness. _____

_____

As honestly as possible, list your seeds of potential. It will help you to discuss this with your workbook companion and your support group before you write.

1. _____
2. _____
3. _____
4. _____
5. _____
6. _____
7. _____
8. _____
9. _____
10. _____

Write out what it would mean in your life to develop the seeds of potential you have listed. _____

_____

_____

_____

Acquiring Knowledge and Skills to Help You Fit In

Wisdom is like honey for your life—if you find it, your future is bright.
—Proverbs 24:14 CEV

What lack of skills is a source of shame for you? _____
_____
_____

What do you do (or what don't you do) in order to hide your lack of skill in this area? _____
_____
_____

Because you feel ashamed, what opportunities do you refuse or cut yourself off from that could help you develop the skills you need? _____
_____
_____

Shame causes you to isolate yourself from others. It makes you ill at ease with individuals and with particular groups in society. In any culture, certain ways of behaving and relating are commonly held to be acceptable. Certain skills enable persons to fit in to whatever community or society of which they are a part. When you are ashamed of yourself and feel that you don't fit in to a society in a meaningful way, you may get caught in a cycle of shame that keeps you from developing the skills you need to be able to fit in.

THE SHAME CYCLE

For some people, this cycle is marked by quiet desperation and the lonely hope that no one will notice that they don't fit in. Some people react in anger and rebellion, fighting against the reality that persons must conform to certain societal norms if they expect to be accepted by others. Whatever your emotional response, the fact remains that in a world where you need to get along with other people, you need to learn the skills to do so.

Dare to learn the skills you lack that will help you fit in to society. Give up your defensive defiance, your retiring helpless position, or your tendency to run away from intimidating situations. The people who function acceptably in society are not better than you; they simply have skills, knowledge, and manners that help them interact successfully with others, which you haven't yet acquired. You can learn to change your behavior.

You break the shame cycle by identifying the skills you lack that trigger shameful feelings and then by learning these skills. You will need courage and determination, but you can find ways to learn these skills without having to admit openly that you lack them. In today's world you can learn things and acquire skills in the privacy of your own home. You can use taped seminars, videotapes, computer networking, correspondence courses, books ordered over the phone, and so on.

Check the following statements that apply to you—there may be several:

___ I want to learn to communicate my ideas and feelings clearly.
___ I want to learn better manners.
___ I want to learn to be a good friend.
___ I want to learn to give and receive love.
___ I want to learn to forgive and accept forgiveness.
___ I want to learn to better take responsibility for my life in the following areas:
    ___ finances
    ___ personal grooming
    ___ spiritual health
    ___ intellectual growth
    ___ managing my home
    ___ caring for my belongings

    ___ _____
    ___ _____

SHAME

___ I want to learn a useful occupation.
___ I want to learn to responsibly handle my role as

    ___ spouse

    ___ parent

    ___ employer/employee

___ I want to learn to set and reach personal goals.
___ I want to learn to get along with others and maintain healthy relationships.

You can seek the advice and support of your workbook companion as well as your support group. Ask for suggestions, tools, and ideas. They will be happy to help you!

Developing Your Unique Talents and Abilities

The expression of your talents will remind you that there is something wonderfully unique about you.—Stephen Arterburn

Expressing a talent is more than something you do; it is an expression of who you are. Venturing to express yourself artistically or creatively and having your artistic expression ridiculed can be a source of shame. One of the best ways to decrease shame is to increase the use of your natural talents. Consider the following example:

Marjorie loved to draw from the time she was a small child. She spent hours on end sketching whatever caught her eye. By the time she started school, she was able to draw quite well and gained a sense of healthy pride from positive feedback given by her teachers. When she entered high school, she fell in love with a young man who was artistically gifted and also quite skilled. She took an art class primarily so that she could be near him. Instead of focusing on her unique talent and developing it, she began to compare her work negatively to his. She showed him her work and looked to him for affirmation. When her romantic intentions were rebuffed, she somehow associated the rejection with a lack of appreciation for her talents. Upon leaving high school, she threw away her art supplies and decided that she wasn't particularly talented after all.

SHAME

Then years later, a friend mentioned that she was taking a painting class and invited Marjorie to join her. The talent was still there. In the supportive environment of a small class, Marjorie blossomed. Her paintings were beautiful. Every time she now looks at the lovely paintings exhibited on the walls of her home and prominently displayed in homes of family and friends, she feels a sense of wonder about herself. The expression of her unique talents reminds her that something is quite special about her.

As a child, what did you love to do, have a strong interest in, or display a special ability for? (Think of things such as art, drama, athletics, music, mechanics, writing, and so on.) _____

_____

_____

Have you ever experienced rejection or ridicule in the area of your talents and abilities? _____

_____

_____

What effect did that rejection or humiliation have on your willingness to develop and use your talents?_____

_____

_____

What is one talent or ability that you were born with? _____

_____

List several ways you could develop or use this talent in some form of creative expression: _____

_____

_____

Here are some guidelines to help you as you pursue your creative gifts:

- Find a supportive environment for your artistic or creative expression.
- Don't get into a situation where your creative expression is being graded or compared to that of others.
- Don't use your creative works or expressions to try to gain the approval of someone whose approval you desperately seek.
- Don't show your creative works to people who have a history of ridiculing you, tearing you down, or criticizing you.
- Find a way to enjoy and appreciate the expression of your talent for the gift that it is.

Finding Fulfillment in Your Work

What you do is valuable; who you are as a person is more valuable.
—Stephen Arterburn

Your work and your worth are closely related. Shame will affect your feelings about your work, and your feelings about your work will affect your sense of shame. Therefore, you need to find a personally fulfilling occupation and do it to the best of your ability.

How does your sense of shame negatively affect your work?

_____

_____

How does your work affect your sense of shame? _____

_____

_____

_____

Does your current job feel shameful to you in some way? Why?

_____

_____

_____

Do you respect the people you associate with at work? If not, how does that affect your self-respect? _____

_____

_____

Do you perform your job to the best of your ability? _____

_____

_____

If you could have any job, what would you like to be doing?

_____

_____

What is stopping you from devising a plan to do what you would most like to do? _____

_____

_____

Do you have a history of job-hopping? If so, how do you think that relates to your sense of shame?_____

_____

_____

You can make changes in your attitude and actions on the job that will reduce your sense of shame. What are they? _____

_____

_____

Coping with Weaknesses

If you accept your limitations you go beyond them.—Brendan Francis

If you live with unhealthy shame, you may have a difficult time acknowledging your weaknesses because weaknesses seem to prove to you that you are deficient as a human being. When you see your weaknesses as proof that you are hopelessly damaged, you won't be motivated to try to change. In contrast, healthy shame allows you to acknowledge your weaknesses without feeling like a failure as a person. The first step toward coping with your weaknesses in a positive way is to acknowledge them.

List weaknesses in yourself that you can now acknowledge:

_____

_____

_____

_____

_____

_____

_____

Now, number them in their order of priority—which ones you want to deal with first, second, third, and so on.

Jesus said that his "strength is made perfect in weakness" (2 Cor. 12:9 NKJV). How can you apply this truth to your areas of weakness? _____

_____

_____

God is patient with us. Are you patient with yourself? Can you think of a time when you have been impatient with yourself, expecting immediate transformation? _____

_____

_____

How might being patient with yourself decrease your sense of shame?

_____

_____

Every human being has weaknesses and strengths. One key to gain emotional wellness is to identify your strengths and put them to use on your own behalf. You may feel weak when you actually have tremendous strength—if you are squandering your strength on just coping with unhealthy life patterns. Consider the following story:

A woman called a radio talk show complaining that she didn't know how to handle her situation. She was married to a very nice man who had a drinking problem. The family, including five children, depended on him for the major part of their finances. Her husband's drinking was a regular part of life, but she said she had managed to "work around" it so it didn't affect the children. Every year or so, her husband would leave unexpectedly and call her from the Bahamas where he had friends and could escape the pressures of family life. Sometimes he would be gone a week, sometimes for months. This time he told the children he would be out for an hour and called a week later to say he would be back in three more weeks.

SHAME

The woman was calling the talk show host in an effort to find out how she could keep from getting angry. (So far she had been able to maintain a loving attitude, hoping that it would help her husband to not feel so pressured and need to escape.) She also wanted to know how she could persuade him to change since nothing she said about his need to stop drinking and stay home had any impact.

The show's host rightly pointed out that she was in denial and suggested she was using her strength ineffectively. It took a tremendous amount of strength for her to maintain a loving attitude when she was suppressing her rightful indignation at her husband's behavior. It took strength to pretend that everything was fine when it wasn't, to continue to convince herself that she could work around her husband's alcoholism and abdication of responsibilities, so that her children were not affected. The host told her the unacceptable behavior would continue as long as she was willing to put up with it and until she began to use her strength effectively.

No one is strong in every area, but you do have strengths as well as weaknesses. Just as others can use their strengths to help where you are weak, your strengths can help others where they are weak.

List areas in which you must be strong to cope:

_____

_____

_____

_____

_____

_____

List ways you could use your strength on your own behalf to move toward emotional wellness: _____

_____

_____

_____

_____

_____

_____

Describe a time when you were strong for someone else who was weak.

_____

_____

Learning to cope with weakness means changing the things about yourself that limit your ability to successfully relate to God, family, friends, and society. Doing this requires making a plan to deal with the weaknesses. List three meaningful goals toward overcoming the weaknesses you just identified:

1. _____

2. _____

3. _____

Adopting New Rituals and Symbols

When you sow an action, you reap a habit. Sow a habit, reap a character. Sow a character, reap a destiny.—Zig Ziglar

A ritual is a repetitive pattern of behavior that has a special meaning associated with it. A symbol is anything you use to represent something or to which you assign significant meaning. Having a morning cup of coffee can be a ritual that is associated with starting a new day, and it can be a symbol of daily order and routine. Rituals and symbols can be either positive or negative, constructive or destructive. If you are working to overcome shame in your life, you need to eliminate rituals and symbols that reinforce your shame, and replace them with positive ones. For example, a man who grew up in poverty always associated tea bags with his shame because his family of twelve would have to share one tea bag on cold mornings when there was nothing to eat. For him, a new symbol that signified his distance from poverty was a fresh tea bag with each cup of tea.

It is not enough to eliminate destructive rituals. You need to adopt new ones that uphold your healthy boundaries and affirm your new way of life. If you feel ashamed of living in a messy home, a new ritual may be clearing the table and washing the dishes after every meal. Here are some other suggestions. Check the ones that may apply to you, then write your own ideas at the end of the list.

__ Attending classes to further your education
__ Making weekly dates with your spouse
__ Having daily quiet time for prayer
__ Attending church or other spiritually uplifting meetings
__ Reading or listening to motivational materials
__ Joining an art class, theater group, or choir
__ Observing a daily grooming regimen
__ Reading bedtime stories to your children
__ Having regular manicures
__ Volunteering for community service

__ _____
__ _____
__ _____

Negative rituals or symbols reinforce unhealthy shame. For example, a person with an overeating problem goes to a donut shop for coffee every morning, can't resist a donut, and then regrets it all day. A person with a drinking problem goes to a bar with his friends after work. A woman with a shopping "addiction" heads for the mall every time she gets off work early. Can you list some negative rituals or symbols that contribute to your sense of shame? List the ritual or symbol, followed by an alternative healthy habit you could replace it with:

Unhealthy Ritual or Symbol   Healthy Habit
_____ / _____
_____ / _____
_____ / _____
_____ / _____
_____ / _____

Treating Yourself
with Respect

No one can make you feel inferior without your consent.
—Eleanor Roosevelt

Shame is characterized by a lack of healthy self-respect. Building a sense of self-respect helps to counteract unhealthy shame. The road to freedom from shame must begin on the solid bedrock of what is true about you, not the shifting sands of how you feel about yourself. The truth is that you are a human being, and as a human being, you are valuable. On the basis of this fact, you take a step of faith. You say to yourself, "Because I am a valuable human being, I choose, as an act of my will, to treat myself with respect." Once you practice treating yourself with respect, the feelings will follow. You will begin to feel more respectable and, therefore, less ashamed.

How can you show yourself respect? Here are some important guidelines. Check the ones that may apply to you. Place a star by the ones that are clearly areas needing work in your life.

___ Keep yourself, your surroundings, and your belongings clean.
___ Establish and maintain order in your life.
___ Behave in ways that are socially acceptable; mind your manners.
___ Dress up and groom yourself to look your best.
___ Exercise, rest, and eat healthfully.

__ Stand up straight, head held high, shoulders back, and smile.

__ Protect your privacy: don't tell everybody your life story.

__ Say no when you mean no.

__ Stop using foul language.

__ Stop putting yourself down and making belittling comments about yourself.

__ Give yourself time each day to have fun and enjoy life.

__ Beautify your surroundings with flowers, fresh paint, music, and/or fragrance.

__ Set a respectful tone in your home: no criticism, mocking, or disrespect.

__ Affirm yourself in areas where others have shamed you.

__ _____

__ _____

Are you willing to practice treating yourself with respect now? Stop reading and do something this very moment that demonstrates treating yourself with respect!

Congratulations! This concludes Part 1 of *The Emotional Freedom Workbook.* Take a moment to write out the three most important lessons you have learned so far about overcoming shame.

1. _____

2. _____

3. _____

Part 2

Unhealthy Relationships

I like doing things for people. I really do. But sometimes I get incredibly tired of it all. I've given so much of myself, yet nobody appreciates me or even says thank you. To be honest, I get the feeling I'm surrounded by people who take and take and never give anything back.—Meredith J.

A word was coined in the late seventies to describe life patterns commonly identified in people having relationships with alcoholics or other addicts. That word—*codependency*—essentially describes a lifestyle in which we focus our attention and life energy on meeting the needs of others, trying to change them, even controlling them while neglecting or avoiding aspects of our own lives in the process. This part of *The Emotional Freedom Workbook* will address these issues.

We are calling this part "Unhealthy Relationships" because codependent patterns of behavior don't always involve others who are addicts and alcoholics.

Some of us immerse ourselves in the lives of our parents, spouses, children, or friends, trying to win their love with our good deeds, hoping—consciously or unconsciously—that they will remain dependent on us so that they will never leave us. In doing so, we are functioning as relationship addicts. As long as we do so, we allow our unhealthy relationships to block our path into emotional freedom.

One woman who facilitates a codependency support group confided that she did not gain power over codependency until she unmasked her real fears. She said, "The turning point came when I realized how selfish my rescuing and controlling behavior was. When I tried to get treatment for my alcoholic son, covered up for him, or tried to control his behavior, the real motivation was that I couldn't bear for anyone to know *my* son was in such a condition. I pretended to offer help for his sake when I was afraid of what people would think of me. I couldn't curb my urge to control his life until I faced off with my deepest fear: being rejected by my peers." Her identity was tied up in her image. If she took her hands off the situation, she might lose her son and risk losing her identity.

What Is Codependency?

I forget what is behind, and I struggle for what is ahead. I run toward the goal, so that I can win the prize . . . that God offers because of what Christ Jesus has done. —Philippians 3:13–14 CEV

Helen and her mother were inseparable—or so it seemed to the casual observer. More accurately, Helen never went anywhere without her mother because she was always trying to pacify the older woman, always trying to solve a "problem," always trying to "make her happy." Betty, Helen's mother, was a chronically depressed woman who controlled her daughter with coldness and disapproval. And Helen, who had always longed to know that her mother really loved her, never stopped trying to satisfy the "needs" of her constantly dissatisfied parent.

At thirty-five years old, Helen met a kindhearted man at her church, and before long, she and Carl were engaged. Carl was amazingly understanding about Helen's seemingly selfless devotion to her mother. He drew the line, however, when Betty tried to manipulate Helen into taking her along on the couple's honeymoon! "Look at it this way, Helen. Your mother will be unhappy wherever she is—with us or here by herself. I want to marry you, not your mom. And you're going to have to stop focusing on her constant demands if our marriage is going to work."

Fortunately, Helen and Carl were able to receive some excellent counseling before their wedding. But for the rest of her mother's life, Helen struggled to overcome her overwhelming need to please her mother and her lifelong habit of trying to earn Betty's elusive love.

The patterns of unhealthy relationships commonly described as codependency are real. However, as with any emerging idea, the concept of codependency can be somewhat confusing. When you hear descriptions of these unhealthy behaviors, you may identify with what is being described and recognize that these behavioral theories relate to your life, but you may not be sure how to apply that understanding in practical ways. This part of *The Emotional Freedom Workbook* will show you how to move from being someone locked into unhealthy relationships to someone who has taken steps to break free from that kind of behavior.

Recovering from codependency does not mean finding a way to change who you are—it is finding a way to accept who you are while learning to live a life of balanced responsibilities. If you start out thinking, *I'm hopelessly addicted to unhealthy relationships; that's just the way I am . . .* , you will be frustrated. But if you start by accepting that you are a person who reacted to life's traumas by neglecting self-care and your own responsibilities while being consumed in someone else's needs, you can find power over codependency without giving up yourself in the process.

You can break free of your compulsion to control and rescue others, and you can dare to reclaim full life for yourself. You will be free to help others, but your help will be offered out of real love, not out of the compulsion that says you have to help or else you will be abandoned. You will be free to say yes and just as free to say no.

Who depends on you emotionally, financially, and in other ways?

_____

_____

_____

_____

UNHEALTHY RELATIONSHIPS

Whom do you try to control, manipulate, rescue, fix, or change?

_____

_____

Describe a time when your involvement in the lives of others left you feeling
used or depleted._____

_____

_____

Describe your reaction to receiving help, compliments, good sensations, and
other nourishing experiences. _____

_____

_____

On a regular basis what do you do for yourself that rejuvenates you—things
such as rest, fun, or creative expression? _____

_____

_____

How do you feel when you say no to a request? _____

_____

_____

The Tree of Your Life

Blessed is the man who trusts in the Lord and has made the Lord his hope and confidence. He is like a tree planted along a riverbank, with its roots reaching deep into the water—a tree not bothered by the heat nor worried by long months of drought. Its leaves stay green and it goes right on producing all its luscious fruit.—Jeremiah 17:7–8 TLB

The life of a codependent person can be represented by a tree. This tree is beautiful. Its great branches stretch toward the sky, providing shade for anyone who would like to rest beneath it. The dense foliage is filled with sounds of birds, squirrels, woodpeckers, and a host of insects that make their home amid the branches and in every available knothole. No one seems to notice that the soil in which the tree is planted has not been tilled or cultivated in ever so long. The roots are stunted; the soil is depleted. Very little nourishment can get through to replenish the life of the tree. The tree takes care of everyone, but no one takes care of the tree. It seems fine. The beauty, the busyness in the branches, and the coolness of the shade—all draw attention away from the tree, which is slowly wasting away from within.

The branches represent areas where you extend yourself into the lives of others. The trunk represents your personal life and inner life. The roots represent your life experiences, beliefs about yourself, and feelings buried in the soil of your past.

A common element of codependency is the need to be socially acceptable at all costs in order to feel okay. You may cover up embarrassing circumstances, protect someone from the consequences of personal behavior, lie, or deny real problems. These actions enable an addict, abuser, or other dependent person to continue a destructive lifestyle without taking responsibility. These actions also protect your image and give you a sense of control and momentary security.

Not all codependency involves direct denial and enabling behavior. You may neglect yourself and be driven to perform. If you doubt your value as a human being, you may find comfort by making yourself available at any hour of the day or night to meet the needs of others. You may struggle with guilt whenever you rest, whenever you say no to a request, or whenever you do something only for yourself.

If you avoid the things in life that trigger overwhelming memories and feelings at the root of who you are, you leave parts of your past untouched, the soil untilled. You say things such as, "What's past is past; there's no good in dredging it up." But the past is not really past if you avoid parts of life today to protect yourself. Avoidance of issues and repression of feelings cut you off from a range of feelings, memories, and activities in your day-to-day life.

Unresolved traumas and losses will powerfully emerge in some form. The adult child of an alcoholic may marry an alcoholic and try to save the spouse the way the person tried to save the alcoholic parent. The person sexually abused as a child may avoid sex altogether by becoming overweight or may display a lack of self-care by becoming indiscriminate about sexual partners. Either way the person has cut off the real intimacy of sex in marriage as it was intended. Another person may refuse to acknowledge a certain holiday because of the death of a loved one at that time of year. Another person may have no conscious memory of past trauma but may experience unexplained physical ailments that act as body clues to the pain of the past.

It's understandable that you would want to numb yourself to the chance of being hurt again. However, this way of dealing with your past shows that the past is not over for you. You feel compelled to maintain your defenses against it without realizing that you are giving up a part of yourself in the process.

As your tree of life continues to grow, the telling moment comes when you must make a choice: Do you dislodge those who have nested there and prune the branches to sustain continued health of the tree? Pruning represents cutting back enough on the control and care of others to give you a chance to replenish your needs. If you are codependent, you forgo pruning for the sake of the nesters. There is no limit to what you are willing to give or endure for the sake of others. You do not sacrifice yourself out of love freely given. Your value, relationships, and security are based on being a nesting place for others. Your identity is the rescuer, savior, martyr, or one who holds things together for everyone else. Perhaps you don't believe the tree deserves a place in the world apart from its usefulness and appearance. Perhaps you fear that if you let go of controlling, manipulating, rescuing, and doing more than enough, the people you love will leave you.

The understanding of what compels you in these ways is probably hidden in the soil of your past, usually your early years of life. Something buried there holds the key to why you focus much of your energy toward others and away from yourself.

The branches represent areas where you extend yourself into the lives of others. Describe some of the "branches" of your tree. _____

_____

_____

The trunk represents your personal life and inner life. Describe the "trunk" of your tree. _____

_____

_____

_____

UNHEALTHY RELATIONSHIPS

The roots represent your life experiences, beliefs about yourself, and feelings buried in the soil of your past. Describe the "roots" of your tree.

_____

_____

The following questions have to do with pruning your tree of life. Please answer them as honestly as possible by circling Y (=Yes) or N (=No):

Is your willingness to give or endure for the sake of others unlimited? Y/N

Do you sacrifice yourself solely out of freely given love? Y/N

Are your relationships, personal value, and security based on your care of others? Y/N

Do you see yourself as a rescuer, savior, martyr, or one who holds things together for others? Y/N

On a separate sheet of paper, draw a picture of what the tree of your life looks like. Make the size of the branches proportionate to your involvement in the lives of others and how much of your life is focused away from yourself. Write in the names of your "nesters." Make the thickness and appearance of the trunk relate to how you secretly feel in terms of personal fulfillment. Make the roots reach out and appear healthy to the degree that you feel you are receiving nourishment for your personal life and inner life. If you know of a particular feeling, past experience, or issue that you have made off-limits, label that root and darken it.

Gaining Power

The courage God gives us is a form of trust in him, knowing that he will be strong, even if we are weak.—Stephen Arterburn

Take time to reflect on the following questions, then answer them as truthfully as you can:

Do you want more out of life than you're getting? Explain.

_____

_____

Do you believe that the world would suffer loss if you started thinking about your own needs and expressing yourself fully? Explain._____

_____

_____

When have you discounted love because you felt it was born out of obligation or because people didn't know the real you? _____

_____

_____

When have you tried to manipulate someone into showing you love? How did the relationship work out? _____

_____

_____

UNHEALTHY RELATIONSHIPS

When you begin to change your codependent lifestyle, which relationships do you suspect will continue, which will be transformed, and which will be lost?

_____

_____

Are any of your present relationships causing you to feel stressed, angry, resentful, bitter, isolated, frustrated, and/or confused? _____

_____

_____

Hard as it is to believe, love is blocked when you live to accommodate and please others. Hiding your true self in an attempt to manage the lives around you gets in the way of love. You give of yourself beyond the call of duty, concluding that after all you have done for others, they will be obligated to give back to you or love you. However, human nature recoils from such pressure and manipulation. You don't get back what you feel is owed, and you resent it. You eventually end up feeling angry or hurt because your giving is unappreciated and taken for granted.

Meanwhile, when an expression of love is offered to you, you may discount it and not be able to receive the real love within your reach. First, since you feel love is owed, you accept it not as an expression of the heart, but as a response born of obligation. The fact that you manipulate responses takes away the joy of being loved. Second, any love you receive is suspect. Since you have revealed only what you think will please people or what you needed to reveal to get your way, you believe the love coming to you is being directed to the image you project, not the real you. To make matters worse, sometimes others will resist your manipulations, refusing to be forced to show love.

As you grow into having healthy relationships, you will learn

- to experience love in greater measure.
- to develop relationships with people who don't need you but love you anyway.

- to transform former "rescuing" relationships into give-and-take situations.
- to make wise choices and accept the consequences of your choices.
- to experience a full range of joyous emotions.

Make a list of things you want out of life that you have not yet pursued because of being caught up in the lives of others:

1. _____
2. _____
3. _____
4. _____
5. _____
6. _____

Make a list of what you fear may happen or what you fear may be lost if you change your codependent habits:

1. _____
2. _____
3. _____
4. _____
5. _____
6. _____

Pruning Back Unhealthy Relational Patterns

. . . we may find ourselves in situations, where we need someone to be there for us, but the person we have chosen cannot or will not do that.
—Melody Beattie

Anyone who has worked with addicts knows it is impossible to recover or to even get to the real issues of life if the person is still using the addictive substance. The alcoholic must stop drinking alcohol. The drug addict must stop using drugs. The compulsive gambler must stop placing bets. With these kinds of addictions, it is easy to see what must be done to begin recovery.

Other people are addicted to things such as food, sex, work, and religion, which are good things, but the "addicts" use them in inappropriate ways. When the misuse or overuse of something good becomes addictive, sobriety is measured by bringing the good thing back into the range of appropriate use. For example, the compulsive overeater can't stop eating altogether; the sex addict need not become celibate; the workaholic needn't quit the job. However, each one must identify and eliminate all excessive and inappropriate use of what has become a form of addiction.

To change unhealthy relationships for the better, you must identify and cut back on inappropriate relational patterns and activities and involvements that act as an escape from your life, while you become overinvolved in the lives of others.

The exercises in this part may seem very difficult to you. They may even seem "wrong" or "un-Christian" even though they are right and godly. Please work with your partner and support group as you reflect on these key questions and needed changes. You may even want to talk to a counselor or therapist. Begin by committing yourself to the following guidelines:

- Take responsibility only for your actions and those of your minor children.
- Do not carry the burden or responsibility for others' problems or consequences of their choices.
- Do not cover up for or lie on behalf of others to protect them from the consequences of their actions.
- At work, pare back to doing what is called for in your assigned job description without jeopardizing your job security.
- Relieve yourself of all nonessential extracurricular involvements for a while. Do what you can to postpone any pressing deadlines.
- Excuse yourself from the expectations of extended family members by explaining that you are in the process of dealing with some significant personal issues.

Again, if you find it impossible to take your mind off others or to limit your focus to your own life even for a brief time, consider seeking the help of professionals who can help you begin the recovery process.

Answer the following questions (exclude involvement in your life or the lives of your minor children, since these are generally appropriate involvements):

Whose problems are you currently worrying about? _____

_____

UNHEALTHY RELATIONSHIPS

Whose life do you currently feel responsible to try to change, fix, control, or rescue from the consequences of personal behavior? _____
_____
_____

Who actively needs your help at this season of time, including groups that ask for or expect your help? _____
_____
_____

What are your current commitments (include home, work, school, friends, social life, and volunteer activities)? _____
_____
_____

What routine duties do immediate family and extended family members expect of you? _____
_____
_____

Compose a list of persons you currently feel responsible for (excepting minor children):

_____ _____ _____
_____ _____ _____
_____ _____ _____
_____ _____ _____

Notify these individuals that you are pruning back on commitment. Let them know they will have to get by for a while without your help. Advise them to make other arrangements as necessary.

If you are married, discuss these steps with your spouse. Explain that you are not going to take a vacation from fulfilling your role in the family, but your change in focus will have an impact. Let your immediate family know that the focus of your attention will be more introspective than usual for a season; that way they won't misinterpret your change in behavior. Ask for their help in allowing you the time and solitude you need to realign your life within healthy relational boundaries.

You may feel that you're "not being nice" when you cut back, but even Jesus Christ recommended occasional times of pruning and he gave a good reason for it. He told his disciples, "I am the true vine, and My Father is the vinedresser. Every branch in Me that does not bear fruit He takes away; and every branch that bears fruit He prunes, that it may bear more fruit" (John 15:1–2 NKJV). With pruning the plant becomes better nourished and ultimately more productive. The same benefits are yours when you prune back involvement in the lives of others.

Write your thoughts about how John 15:1–2 applies to your relationships and the work you are doing to prune the "tree" of your life. _____

_____

_____

_____

The Focus Is on You

God loved you before you were born, when you were only a thought in his mind.—Stephen Arterburn

Emily entered an inpatient treatment program for depression after discovering that her "perfect" husband, Bill, struggled with sex addiction and had been involved in pornography, numerous affairs, and indiscriminate sexual encounters. She didn't consider herself "depressed," but if that's what they wanted to call her, she would go along with it. What she really wanted to do was to gain insight into helping her husband. He was the one with the problem. She was obsessed with understanding what could cause such behavior, discovering how she could make sure he never acted out again, and finding out if his compulsive behavior was somehow her fault.

The first few days in the hospital Emily struggled with the thought that maybe there was something wrong with her. Surely if she had been a good enough wife, this wouldn't have happened. That was what people had intimated. Maybe she wasn't attractive enough. Maybe she wasn't adventurous enough sexually. She saw herself as intricately connected with Bill's problem. She saw herself as both the cause and the cure. She didn't consider ending the relationship—she couldn't conceive of living without him. Anyway, the situation could work to her advantage. If she stood by him and helped him get through this problem, he would never dare to leave her.

The therapist asked Emily to talk about herself. At first she recounted her qualifications and achievements as though she were interviewing for a job or trying to favorably impress a date. "What about the painful areas of your life before this crisis?" asked the doctor. "Tell me about you and your life history. Especially highlight the parts you don't like to talk about."

"Oh, that . . . ," Emily quietly replied. Then with a frozen expression on her face, she blandly recounted a series of traumatic experiences within her family of origin: adultery, death threats, suicide attempts, alcoholism, drug abuse, physical violence, poverty, imprisonment, untimely deaths, abandonment, compulsive gambling, overdoses, attempted murders, and incest.

In treatment Emily learned to deal with her feelings related to what Bill had done. She came to accept that his addiction was his problem and his recovery was his domain. She made a commitment to let go of all the manipulations she used to guarantee his dependence on her, choosing to stay in the relationship out of love rather than fear.

Emily was also safely guided in dealing with the emotional debris of her life. As the therapists helped her face the feelings that seemed too much to bear, she began to see patterns in her life. She came to understand that she transferred attention away from herself as a means of coping and she established relationships with people who seemed to need her strength so that she could manipulate and control. She realized that she scouted for neediness in others as an opportunity to tie them to her. In that way she lessened the possibility of being abandoned as she had been as a child. Her desperate fear of abandonment made relationships based on being needed a "safe" substitute for the risk of real love.

Compare the elements of the story about Emily with your own life. What parallels can you find regarding your thoughts and feelings about yourself and the person or persons you are trying to control, fix, or change? How do you feel when you move closer to dealing with issues in your life? Journal your thoughts.

_____

_____

UNHEALTHY RELATIONSHIPS

_____

_____

When did you *first* become consumed with thinking about another person's behavior: focusing your attention on how you could change it, what you could do to control it, or what you may have done to cause it? _____

_____

_____

What was your life like during that time? _____

_____

_____

When you recount painful events that have happened in your life, are you disconnected from your emotions?_____

_____

Do you have blank spots in your memory—spans of time you cannot recall?

_____

Do you have selective memory, able to recall only positive experiences, when you suspect there is more to the story? _____

_____

Have you ever justified neglecting or avoiding your problems and responsibilities because they seemed small in comparison to the problems and needs of others? Explain. _____

_____

Have you ever kept account of the way you supported others in their times of need as an emotional insurance policy to bind them to you for life? Explain.

_____

_____

Jesus said, "Why do you look at the speck in your brother's eye, but do not consider the plank in your own eye? Or how can you say to your brother, 'Let me remove the speck from your eye'; and look, a plank is in your own eye? Hypocrite! First remove the plank from your own eye, and then you will see clearly to remove the speck from your brother's eye" (Matt. 7:3–5 NKJV).

Write out how you think this Scripture applies to relationships where you focus on others' problems instead of your own._____

_____

_____

List three problem areas in your life that you have minimized or ignored while you have focused your attention on others:

1. _____
2. _____
3. _____

List three circumstances or events in your life history that would understandably cause difficult emotions, which you recall with little or no emotion:

1. _____
2. _____
3. _____

List three ways you involve yourself in the lives of others while your own issues go unattended:

1. _____
2. _____
3. _____

Inner Versus
Outward Direction

If you do not live the life you believe
You will believe the life you live.—Zig Ziglar

One characteristic that is common to all unhealthy relationships is living life directed by external cues rather than internal cues. That way of life needs to be corrected to gain power over codependency. The following illustration may help you identify that type of behavior in your life.

Suppose you joined a choir because you wanted to sing and perform. The proper way to prepare is to learn your part as the notes, rhythm, melody, and harmony are written. But let's suppose that you joined the choir and began performing without ever having heard the music and without ever having learned your part. In fact, suppose you don't know how voices blend together to create harmony. Nevertheless, you are thrilled to be a part of the choir, and you sing out enthusiastically. But you don't sing the right notes. And you get an immediate response from those around you. The choristers stare at you. "You're off-key," one whispers. "Sing higher!" another says. You try to sing higher. After a few adjustments of pitch, the critical looks of the others melt into expressions of relief. After a while you develop the ability to adjust your singing to the silent glances and hand motions of those around you. Sometimes, because you fear rejection, you move your lips without making a sound. You learn that whenever you want to sing, you must sing according to the dictates of others.

In this example, singing can represent your desire to live to your full potential and to be accepted, and the choir can represent your family of origin. Someone in your family should have helped you learn a healthy way to live, defined by set values, moral guidelines, and life-giving principles.

If your family life was troubled, however, you may not have been informed that there was any other way to live. You may always have had the desire to sing the song of life, but you may not have known the tune and may not have believed you had the capacity to learn. The only way you learned to live was by changing your performance in response to the reactions of family members. Your survival may have depended on your ability to read the cues of those around you and adjust your behavior until their disapproval was appeased. Sometimes that may have meant you didn't sing the song of life at all, that you just went through the motions, pretending to be what you thought they wanted you to be.

If you grew up in a highly controlled or even repressive family system, your family may not have been able to lead you into a healthy life because of their own problems. Instead of freeing you to express yourself, their rules may have stifled the true expression of your feelings, thoughts, opinions, desires, perceptions, and talents. The way you learned to survive in your family of origin isn't the best way to live a healthy life. This realization gives you the opportunity to grasp the joy of living that has been stifled.

On a scale of 1 to 10, rate the degree to which you were controlled by trying to please or appease others as a child. Mark the following scale accordingly.

1 means completely controlled   10 means free to express inner self

1_____10

On the same scale, rate the way you live your life now.

1 means completely controlled   10 means free to express inner self

1_____10

UNHEALTHY RELATIONSHIPS

List the names of persons in your childhood for whom you adjusted your behavior to please or appease:

1. _____
2. _____
3. _____
4. _____

List the names of persons you currently try to please or appease:

1. _____
2. _____
3. _____
4. _____

Do you know someone who best serves as an example of living a healthy life? Name the person and explain why you believe this to be true.

_____

_____

Finding the
Missing Pieces

Pain never enters a person's life without God's permission.
—Stephen Arterburn

Somewhere inside you is a collection of memories, feelings, pleasures, hopes, and dreams that have been lost to you. Dealing with certain areas of life triggers fearful emotions, reminds you of your stormy past, or stirs up feelings that life is dangerously out of control. You don't make a conscious choice to shut off the feelings or refuse to deal with those areas of life. You just avoid them. Perhaps you grew up in severe poverty; therefore, dealing with finances is emotionally overwhelming to you. Perhaps your parents continually fought and argued, and you are unable to cope with raised voices, angry words, or emotional tension. Perhaps your brother or sister was always favorably compared to you, and you recoil from any "competitive" situation. Perhaps you were abused by a family member or friend, and now you find emotional and/or sexual intimacy dangerous.

Here's an example: Ralph's father was a compulsive gambler. Ralph grew up hearing promises of a bright future with lots of money. Each time Daddy left for the racetrack, he said, "If I win today, I'll bring you a present," or "When we hit it big, we can have a big house, and maybe we can get you a pony."

In real life there was never enough money to pay the bills. The phone was disconnected. As a teenager, Ralph used the phone booth to call friends, and he made up excuses to cover his shame. Creditors were at the door. Daddy made

Ralph tell them he wasn't home. When the school year began, they couldn't afford new clothes, so Ralph made the best of what he could find at a thrift store. The family eventually lost their modest home, and when Daddy died, they borrowed money to bury him.

It's not clear when it happened, but at some time Ralph tossed away hopes of financial security. As an adult, he became successful in his career, but he refused to deal with financial matters. Sometimes he didn't pay bills because he avoided looking at them. His wife usually handled the money. Thinking about money, either having it or not having it, made him uncomfortable, so he abandoned that part of his life. It took a crisis—a financial collapse coupled with seeing his own children begin to worry over financial insecurity—before Ralph would face that part of his life.

Anything that brings you back to the lost areas of yourself may be tremendously intimidating, but it offers you a wonderful opportunity to reclaim your life and realize that you can handle uncomfortable issues, one by one. After discussing the following questions with your workbook companion, answer them as well as you can.

What is there about your life—past or present—that you don't want to think about or talk about? _____

_____

_____

_____

List anything you are aware of that is missing from your life, holding you back from a whole and satisfying life: _____

_____

_____

_____

You can successfully reclaim each lost area of your life and have a fresh start. You can face whatever troubling emotions are associated with these elements of life, take responsibility for your life, and enjoy the benefits. With that in mind, rewrite the list you just made from a different perspective. What are some things you would *want* (if you allowed yourself to want) to make your life fulfilling?

_____

_____

_____

_____

Doing this exercise may arouse buried emotions. What are the feelings associated with each item you listed? _____

_____

If you are angry, does the anger protect you from the more overwhelming feelings of fear and sadness? _____

_____

Do you feel any desperation at the thought of dealing with these issues that you have avoided for so long? _____

_____

Is it hard for you to turn your deficits into desires? Why? _____

_____

_____

Take a Look at Your Physical Life

Confrontation doesn't always bring a solution to the problem, but until you confront the problem, there will be no solution.—James Baldwin

Areas of everyday life that would usually be nonthreatening can become associated with danger or emotional pain. When this happens, your self-preservation instinct warns you to stay away from whatever you have associated with further danger. Things that would normally elicit no particular response become flares marking where a painful experience has occurred and directing you to detour around the debris of whatever caused your pain.

You are now going to undertake a portion of your journey where you will sort out for yourself precisely what you are avoiding in your life and what this emotional debris points to that needs to be cleared up.

First consider your physical life. Go over these lists of items that are part of normal physical behavior and self-care. Rate on a scale of 1 to 10 how well you care for yourself in these ways (1 means not caring for yourself at all; 10 means consistent self-care). Be truthful and be specific. Place a check next to any area of physical self-care that you do not perform on a regular basis.

Health and Safety   Rating

1. Maintain a safe environment at home, work, and play.   _____

2. Obey safety rules at home, work, and play.   _____

3. Protect yourself from those who would do you harm.   _____

4. Learn and practice self-protection skills relative to the level of danger in your environment.   _____

5. Practice preventive medical care on a regular basis (get annual medical checkup; follow doctor's orders).   _____

6. Practice preventive dental care on a regular basis (get checkup every six months).   _____

7. Protect your sexual boundaries. See yourself as a sexual person designed for meaningful relationship rather than a sexual object to be used to satisfy someone else's sexual desires.   _____

8. Eat a healthy and balanced diet.   _____

9. Allow yourself enough privacy to maintain dignity.   _____

10. Allow yourself needed amounts of rest to maintain peak performance (approximately eight hours of sleep nightly, quiet times while awake, one day of rest each week, annual vacations).   _____

11. Follow routine care for maintaining the health of each part of your body. (For example, if you wear contact lenses, do you regularly clean, disinfect, and care for them? Do you provide yourself with proper footwear to give your feet support and protection?)   _____

12. Trace down unexplained chronic physical conditions (these are sometimes physical clues to repressed traumas).   _____

13. Take medication as prescribed by doctor.   _____

14. Care for personal hygiene as appropriate for your physical condition. Attend to any physical problems or health problems related to your sex organs. (This is important, because treating

your sex organs differently from other parts of your body may indicate some sort of sexual abuse.)   _____

15. Exercise aerobically to develop strength and coordination.   _____

16. Keep your living space reasonably clean and orderly.   _____

17. Enjoy the full use of all your senses without isolating yourself from some facet of life: hearing, smelling, tasting, touching, seeing, and enjoying your sexuality.   _____

18. Satisfy your appetite for food and drink regularly in healthy ways rather than live in a cycle of self-deprivation, binges, and guilt.   _____

Physical Grooming   Rating

1. Shower or bathe daily.   _____

2. Wash your hands before eating and after using the bathroom.   _____

3. Style and groom hair attractively every day.   _____

4. Wash your hair regularly.   _____

5. Brush teeth two to three times daily; floss daily.   _____

6. Groom fingernails and toenails regularly.   _____

7. Provide yourself with clothing that is appropriate to the climate and socially acceptable.   _____

8. Wear neat and clean clothing every day.   _____

9. Wear cosmetics, fragrance, or aftershave if you choose.   _____

10. Treat yourself to little extras that enhance your appearance and make you feel better about yourself, such as accessories, jewelry, a new tie, a new hairstyle, manicures, facials, etc.   _____

Environment and Possessions   Rating

1. Buy yourself clothing as needed. (Take note if you feel more comfortable buying clothing for others than you do for yourself,

and specify any particular items of clothing you don't buy for yourself.) _____

2. Care for clothing in a responsible manner: regular laundering, mending, pressing, hanging up in closet, etc. _____

3. Create a home environment that provides for your particular needs and the needs of your family. _____

4. Establish a routine to maintain home environment you have created: make beds, wash dishes, vacuum floors, dust furniture, present attractive meals (note any areas of home care that cause you to procrastinate or feel ashamed). _____

5. Establish and enforce boundaries that maintain the safety, beauty, order, and comfort of your home to meet the needs of your family. (This includes not tolerating violence, substance abuse, and other out-of-control behavior in your home. It also includes limiting your commitments so you can spend time with your family and meet one another's legitimate needs.) _____

6. Create and maintain a work or school environment that serves your needs and is orderly and attractive. _____

7. Buy things that appeal to your senses in a positive way: fragrances for body and home, music, artwork, interior decorating items, foods and drinks you love, fabrics that are pleasant to the touch, etc. _____

8. Take responsibility for maintaining your possessions. (For example, do you keep your car clean inside and out? Do you read the manuals for appliances and take care of them as instructed?) _____

9. Get repairs whenever something breaks or is damaged. _____

For all the items you rated 5 or lower, write a letter in the margin to designate the following: an *N* if this is something you neglect; an *A* if this is something you avoid; an *R* if this is something for which you refuse to take responsibility; a *C* if this is not something missing but something you rigidly control. Be as specific and honest as possible.

Here is how to determine which category applies:

Place it in the *N* (neglected) category if it doesn't seem important and holds no emotional intensity when you think about it. It just isn't a priority.

Place it in the *A* (avoided) category if it is something you feel uncomfortable with or procrastinate over, or it holds some level of emotional intensity.

Place it in the *R* (refused) category if it is something you have thought about and acknowledge that it should be accepted as your responsibility, but for some reason, you have exempted yourself from taking responsibility.

Place it in the *C* (rigidly controlled) category if you feel a sense of compulsion over that area of life, such as feeling driven to keep your home spotless, compulsively washing your hands, or otherwise being driven in that area.

Consider the patterns you notice related to taking care of yourself physically. Is there anything in your upbringing or past experience that might affect the areas where you do not take care of yourself or where you exert rigid control? Write your thoughts about your neglected areas and your rigidly controlled areas regarding what they may have to do with your past. _____

_____

_____

_____

Take a Look at Your Emotional Life

You shall know the truth, and the truth shall make you free.
—Jesus Christ

Emotions can appear as formidable enemies when you are living in a situation that is out of control, especially if you experienced similar circumstances as a child. Feelings of powerlessness, deep shame, abandonment, foreboding, loneliness, self-loathing, hatred, terror, desperation, and their kin haunt the inner rooms of your soul if you have been overpowered by painful experiences.

You are not the only one who has preserved a sense of safety by learning not to feel too much. The uniqueness of your circumstances and the emotional "ghosts" lurking within your heart do not need to be compared to anyone else's. However, you need to face your feelings in order to develop healthy relationships.

Rate yourself on a scale of 1 to 10 for each item (1 means this is never true of you; 10 means this is always true of you).

Current Emotional Health   Rating

1. Able to feel, express, and accept the entire spectrum of emotions: sadness, happiness, fear, anger, jealousy, envy, and their various manifestations.   _____

UNHEALTHY RELATIONSHIPS

2. Able to accept expression of the entire range of emotions in others, especially your children and spouse. _____

3. Respond with emotional intensity appropriate to the situation (as opposed to overreacting or not feeling anything when it would be normal to feel something). _____

4. Attach the emotional reaction to the true source (as opposed to transferring your emotional intensity to someone who did not prompt your emotions and does not deserve your intense reaction; for example, blowing up at your child when you are angry with your spouse but feel unable to express your anger to your spouse). _____

5. Able to enjoy what is joyful in the current moment (without obsessing about what might happen to snatch the joy away). _____

6. Allow others to feel whatever they are feeling without having to take responsibility for causing their emotions or needing to try to change what they are feeling to make them feel better. _____

7. Able to experience intimacy with persons close to you; to share deeply from your heart; to reveal your strengths and weaknesses; to accept their self-revelations, strengths, and weaknesses. _____

8. Able to relate comfortably with others who are different from you (age, social status, financial status, education, and so on). _____

9. Able to grieve your losses and move beyond them. _____

10. Able to trust when trust is warranted. _____

11. Able to talk about feelings and to have feelings proportionate to what you think and feel. _____

12. Able to visit locations, symbols, or mementos of past pain without being emotionally devastated or numb. _____

13. Able to comfort others, being compassionate rather than controlling or judgmental. _____

14. Able to be alone without being overwhelmed with loneliness. _____

15. Derive pleasure from reality (of past, present, and future hopes) rather than from fantasy that is out of sync with reality. _____

Emotionally Nourishing Choices   Rating

1. Willing to take responsibility for your own emotional health even if you are not responsible for what caused the pain. _____

2. Ask for what you believe will help you feel better, and keep asking and seeking until you find what you need. _____

3. Take actions that lead toward emotional health and balance. _____

4. Remove yourself from relationships and situations that are hurtful to you over and over again in the same ways. _____

5. Do for yourself the things that were neglected in your childhood. _____

6. Stop doing to yourself the things that have caused you pain and continue to cause you pain. _____

7. Develop relationships with persons who love and respect you as a valuable human being. _____

8. Make choices, commitments, and plans that lead to emotional health and healing of emotional wounds. _____

9. Admit when you cannot resolve emotional problems, and seek appropriate help until emotional balance is restored. _____

10. Participate in a network of people committed to giving and receiving emotional nourishment. _____

Dealing with Emotional Pain of the Past — Rating

1. Acknowledge your pain; share with someone supportive; validate and treat hurts and emotional wounds so they can heal. _____

2. Identify and grieve losses. _____

3. Resolve unforgiveness, bitterness, and resentment. _____

4. Acknowledge the true facts of happenings that hurt you; end denial (of the who, what, when, where, and why of your emotional wound). _____

5. Reexamine childhood beliefs about yourself and your life (formed in reaction to past abuse, deception, neglect, or victimization) in light of adult understanding. _____

6. Challenge old beliefs and replace them with beliefs that affirm your true value as a human being. _____

7. Express, analyze, and understand repressed emotions. _____

8. Establish new symbols to remind you of the truth about your value and your life. _____

Now look over the list, and note items after which you wrote the lowest numbers. Pick the three that you feel would best help you at this time and list them:

1. _____

2. _____

3. _____

Think of times when you actually made those choices, and describe the results.

_____

_____

_____

_____

Describe how your current situation could be improved by making those choices.

_____

_____

_____

What seems to keep you from making those choices? _____

_____

_____

Write about the most glaring item from your past that has not yet been dealt with according to the items listed under "Dealing with Emotional Pain of the Past." _____

_____

_____

After prayerful reflection, describe the feelings that you don't allow yourself to feel. _____

_____

_____

_____

How do you suppress emotions? _____

_____

_____

What Do You Believe About Yourself?

Test my thoughts and find out what I am like.—Psalm 26:2 CEV

Your belief structure is a key player in developing unhealthy relationships. Your mind developed beliefs and assumptions you could use to gain a sense of security in the face of danger. Perhaps you believed that if you were a better student or if you made yourself useful and relieved some of the pressure at home, Dad wouldn't drink or Mom wouldn't fly into a rage. Maybe you thought that if you never made mistakes, Dad wouldn't criticize you or Mom wouldn't constantly compare you unfavorably to others.

The beliefs you established gave you an illusion of safety—control over the dangers of life. You drew conclusions about what left you vulnerable, then used those conclusions to determine what you could do to try to make sure you were safe. Some of the tactics you developed for survival may have included these:

- Creating a false image of yourself
- Obeying "don't talk, don't trust, don't feel"
- Observing superstitions
- Trying to be perfect
- Manipulating and/or yielding to an abuser

These tactics, based on childhood beliefs, probably worked for a while. However, the same beliefs that helped you survive then may hurt your relationships now.

When beliefs are based on a child's perspective, they are not based on reality. In reality, what you were taught about life may not have been right or true. In reality, neither were you responsible for nor could you have controlled the people around you. What was done to you had very little to do with the kind of person you are. It had everything to do with the kind of people you were dependent on—their conditions, addictions, and compulsions.

Today, in the hope of protecting yourself, you may still be living by beliefs that needlessly deprive you of intimacy, trust, friendships, good feelings, rest, peace of mind, and more. You may seek to control, manipulate, rescue, and fix others in your quest for security, but controlling others is impossible. Life is not—nor will it ever be—completely within your control. You can know greater hope of security only by reevaluating the beliefs that are foundational to your unhealthy relationships and challenging them.

The beliefs you hold about yourself will affect the way you behave. In order to protect yourself, you have probably established a number of "emotional safety rules" that you developed to keep you out of harm's way.

Here are examples of "rules" people develop to help themselves feel safe:

- "If I am a good person and always try to do what is right, bad things won't happen to me."
- "If I never open up to anyone or trust anyone, I will not get hurt."
- "If I don't let my feelings surface, they can't hurt me."
- "If I keep my distance from people, I'll be safe."

Do any of these statements sound like something you might think? What are your top three "emotional safety rules"?

1. _____
2. _____
3. _____

Are these rules based on sound beliefs? Explain. _____

_____

UNHEALTHY RELATIONSHIPS

Do they work for you? Explain._____
_____
_____

In what ways do they limit your full enjoyment of life? _____
_____
_____

Which of these rules do you need to change? _____
_____
_____

You were clearly reacting to something when you made safety rules for yourself. Allow yourself time to reflect on your childhood, then complete the following sentences from the perspective you had as a child:

The most overpowering experience of my life was _____
_____
_____.

In order to survive, I believed I had to _____
_____
_____.

I thought that I could keep the danger of being overpowered again away if I would _____
_____.

In order to stay safe, I gave up _____
_____.

In order to stay safe, I tried to control _____

_____

_____.

Putting your thoughts in writing may already have helped you understand your present patterns of behavior. It's important for you to understand that when you change your beliefs, you will change your life.

Mental, Spiritual, and Financial Warning Signs

If you are already wise, you will become even wiser.
And if you are smart, you will learn to understand.—Proverbs 1:5 CEV

You could say that your intellectual capacities are the brains behind "Operation Survival" or "Operation Striving to Please." You must have figured out how to cope to become a person others depend on when they are in need. However, you may be able to identify warning signs in the mental, spiritual, and financial areas of life that indicate unhealthy relationships. Some signs of healthy mental and intellectual life are included here. Consider to what degree these are operating in your life and in what specific ways you are missing out on full health. Try to rate your thoughts as you read the following statements using a scale of 1 through 10 (1 means you never think this way; 10 means you think this way most of the time).

Indicators of Healthy Mental Life   Rating

1. Aware of and accept reality. _____

2. Open to new ideas and willing to consider new information to refine beliefs; continually learning and growing. _____

3. Able to balance rational understanding of life with emotional, physical, and spiritual realities. _____

4. Aware of reasonable limits and seek to live within them (for example, don't believe "I can't do anything!" but acknowledge, "I can do anything within my realistic limitations"). _____

5. See life as a continuum between two poles rather than all-or-nothing, black or white, perfection or failure; have self-image that is neither grandiose nor self-negating. _____

6. Able to direct thoughts and imagination in healthy ways rather than be consumed with worry, fears, and obsession with the lives of others. _____

If you rated some of these items 5 or lower, list specific examples of how they negatively affect your life: _____

_____

_____

_____

Describe alternative ways of thinking you could develop to counteract these unhealthy patterns. _____

_____

_____

Did this exercise make you feel defensive? Explain. _____

_____

_____

Sometimes unhealthy patterns in relationships carry over into the relationship with God. Unhealthy relationships may be affecting your spiritual life. In the following ratings, you will identify areas of spirituality you may want to take hold of as well as spiritual problems you may choose to correct.

Rate the following statements of spiritual health on a scale of 1 to 10 (1 means you don't have this experience; 10 means this is a regular part of your spiritual experience).

Signs of Spiritual Health   Rating

1. Secure in God's everlasting love for you. _____

2. Confident that there are a purpose and a plan for your life. _____

3. Able to rest in the knowledge that your relationship with God is founded on love rather than dependent on your ongoing performance. _____

4. Able to trust God to take care of you and your loved ones. _____

5. Able to follow through on spiritual disciplines (prayer, meditation, worship, sharing your faith, studying Scripture, obedience) from an internal desire to know, love, and please God, not from an external demand to maintain God's favor. _____

6. Experience the peace that comes from within and remains with you even during trying circumstances. _____

7. Acknowledge your need for God; don't assume God's need for you. _____

8. Able to receive forgiveness (can admit sin, failings, errors, willful acts of rebellion) and extend forgiveness to others. _____

9. Able to live according to your beliefs: having words and deeds that match. _____

10. Practice humility rather than present a list of spiritual credentials; admit when you fall short rather than pretend to be perfect. _____

Spiritual Problems Typical of Those Addicted to Unhealthy Relationships

Rating

1. Blame God for not protecting you from whatever overwhelmed you. _____

2. Suspect that God cannot be depended on in times of need and that the only person you can rely on is yourself. _____

3. Feel responsible for the survival of others, playing a godlike role in their lives. _____

4. Believe you know the will of God for others. _____

5. Feel it is your responsibility to enforce God's will upon others, or to cause them to obey him. _____

6. Sincerely doubt that God's will can be carried out in the lives of people you care about if you don't do your part. _____

7. Believe you must maintain a "spiritual" image of perfection because you don't want God to get a bad reputation (you are his personal representative). _____

8. Believe you must maintain an image of spiritual perfection because your relationship with God will be damaged if you don't. _____

9. See yourself on a spiritual plane higher than the one most people are on. _____

10. Console yourself for your imperfections by judging others who are "much worse than you." _____

11. Believe your religion is a burden to bear; believe God imposes the same rules on you that you impose on yourself. _____

12. Think that prayer is a wrestling match in which you attempt to gain control of God to get him to do what you know should be done. _____

Describe the spiritual problems you discovered in the ratings. Explain what you could do to start to change them._____

_____

_____

What do you think would happen if you let go of your spiritual life and the spiritual lives of others into God's hands? _____

_____

_____

What do you think would happen if you invited God to reveal himself to you as he is? _____

_____

_____

Jeremiah 29:11–13 states, "'For I know the plans that I have for you,' declares the LORD, 'plans for welfare and not for calamity to give you a future and a hope. Then you will call upon Me and come and pray to Me, and I will listen to you. And you will seek Me and find Me, when you search for Me with all your heart'" (NASB). Do you believe that God's plans for you are good? You may have difficulty seeing "a future and a hope." If so, stop to write a prayer. Express your real feelings, doubts, and needs, seeking God with your *whole* heart.

_____

_____

_____

God's Word also says, "And we know that all that happens to us is working for our good if we love God and are fitting into his plans" (Rom. 8:28 TLB). Even though we don't know exactly *how* God is working things out for the best, we can believe he is doing so. What are some of the negative things in your life that you look forward to seeing him work out for the best? _____

_____

_____

The way you deal with your finances will show you what you value, how well you take responsibility for your life, and how you may be trying to control others. Rate your financial health on a scale of 1 to 10 (1 means you never do this; 10 means you do this regularly). Place a check next to the items you don't handle responsibly on a regular basis.

Typical Financial Responsibilities   Rating

1. Live within a realistic budget.   _____
2. Know current assets and debts; keep a running account.   _____
3. Plan for financial security in case of future cash-flow problems.   _____
4. Maintain checking account and regularly balance the figures.   _____
5. Spend only available funds.   _____
6. Develop skills and use abilities to be gainfully employed.   _____
7. Have clearly defined personal goals and priorities that lead to financial stability.   _____
8. Provide basic necessities for self and dependent children through work or other available resources.   _____

Possible Financial Indicators of Unhealthy Relationships   Rating

1. Feel guilty whenever buying something for yourself.   _____
2. Feel guilty whenever buying something at full price.   _____

UNHEALTHY RELATIONSHIPS

3. Spend discretionary income on others while your legitimate needs are left unattended. _____

4. Feel unable to order what you really want while eating out and instead order something inexpensive. _____

5. Spend or gamble money indiscriminately (since you believe there will never be enough to get what you need anyway). _____

6. Go without things you need even though you have the money to buy them. _____

7. Avoid getting medical care for yourself because you don't want to spend money on yourself. _____

8. Consider spending money on your needs and wants to be a waste. _____

9. Feel you have to apologize, hide, or make excuses for anything you get for yourself, especially anything nice. _____

10. Say you don't care about having nice things as long as others in your family do. _____

11. Avoid fulfilling your earning potential because you can't conceive of spending money on yourself and don't want the responsibility of deciding where to spend the money. _____

12. Spend compulsively on things to make yourself look presentable to the outside world. _____

13. Feel covetous and envious of anyone who has more than you because you feel your worth is judged by what you have, how you look, and other externals. _____

14. Pretend to have more money than you do. _____

15. Rigidly control the finances of others or use money as a tool to manipulate them. _____

16. Take financial responsibility for others who should bear the weight themselves. _____

Identify three of the financial indicators of unhealthy relationships that apply to you. Describe how they are manifest in your life.

1. _____
2. _____
3. _____

Turn each problem into a statement of how you want to change to correct the problem.

1. _____
2. _____
3. _____

What feelings arose as you considered your financial life? _____
_____
_____

What are you afraid will happen if you stop rescuing people who have become financially dependent on you? _____
_____
_____

Discuss your intellectual, spiritual, and financial indicators and goals for change with your workbook partner. Ask for the help and encouragement to follow through with the changes you need to make.

Rediscovering Talents, Treasures, and Dreams

There is so much more to life than guarding your heart!
There is so much more to you than the pain you are dodging!
—Connie Neal

You are a unique human being, created by God with a special purpose. If you grew up in unhealthy relationships—always trying to be the person you had to be to survive—you may not know who you really are. You may have lost sight of your talents. Part of recovering from unhealthy relationships is rediscovering your talents, treasures, and dreams.

David wrote,

You made all the delicate, inner parts of my body, and knit them together in my mother's womb. Thank you for making me so wonderfully complex! It is amazing to think about. Your workmanship is marvelous—and how well I know it. You were there while I was being formed in utter seclusion! You saw me before I was born and scheduled each day of my life before I began to breathe. Every day was recorded in your Book! (Ps. 139:13–16 TLB)

This Scripture applies to every person.

How does your view of yourself agree or disagree with God's view of you as expressed in these verses? _____

_____

_____

If you grew up in an overly controlling family or a family that struggled with drug or alcohol abuse, your talents, treasures, and dreams were probably discounted or even forbidden. When life is consumed with surviving, there is little done to nurture the heartfelt desires of a child. Now that you are an adult, you can give yourself permission to pursue your talents, treasures, and dreams. Gaining power over an addiction to unhealthy relationships involves living to the best of your abilities, no matter what has happened to you in the past. You can step out of the past and into the future by rediscovering your talents, treasures, and dreams.

Talents are your inborn, God-given abilities. You may have a talent for art, music, athletics, mathematics, writing, dance, drama, and so on. List at least five talents that you think you have:

1. _____
2. _____
3. _____
4. _____
5. _____
6. _____
7. _____

Treasures are your favorite things—things you value for whatever reasons or for no particular reason. A treasure is a treasure simply because you appreciate it.

UNHEALTHY RELATIONSHIPS

List at least ten things you treasure—possessions, experiences, foods, events, books, ideas, or anything else that is an expression of your personal taste:

1. _____ 7. _____
2. _____ 8. _____
3. _____ 9. _____
4. _____ 10. _____
5. _____ 11. _____
6. _____ 12. _____

Dreams are what you would wish for yourself if you dared. Dreams hold tremendous power when they are used to envision a healthier and happier way of life. A dream is an emotional investment in what you would hope for yourself if you allowed yourself the privilege of hoping. You may have experienced such devastation and disappointments that you are afraid to dream great dreams. If that is the case, reflect deeply on the following exercise: If you weren't afraid of disappointment, what would your best dreams be? List at least five:

1. _____
2. _____
3. _____
4. _____
5. _____
6. _____
7. _____

Your talents, treasures, and dreams can lie dormant for your entire life if you don't take action to develop, experience, pursue, and enjoy them. Will you dare to develop your talents? Will you choose to give yourself the gift of enjoying your treasures? Will you risk pursuing your long-lost dreams? Write your thoughts about what you could do differently—beginning today—about your talents, treasures, and dreams. _____

_____

_____

_____

_____

Accepting Full Responsibility for Your Life

You may have been someone else's victim in the past, but if you refuse to take responsibility for solving your problems today, you continue to victimize yourself.—Connie Neal

Many people with a tendency toward unhealthy relationships have a difficult time accepting themselves as a combination of good and bad. They see themselves alternatively either as perfect or terrible, good or bad, invincible or utterly defeated. It can be helpful to take a brief inventory of your assets and liabilities, so you can learn to live with both.

Good Things About My Character

1. _____
2. _____
3. _____
4. _____
5. _____

Bad Things About My Character

1. _____
2. _____

3. _____

4. _____

5. _____

Good Things About My Body or Appearance

1. _____

2. _____

3. _____

4. _____

5. _____

Bad Things About My Body or Appearance

1. _____

2. _____

3. _____

4. _____

5. _____

Good Things About My Personality

1. _____

2. _____

3. _____

4. _____

5. _____

Bad Things About My Personality

1. _____

2. _____

3. _____

4. _____

5. _____

UNHEALTHY RELATIONSHIPS

Past Victories

1. _____
2. _____
3. _____
4. _____
5. _____

Past Losses

1. _____
2. _____
3. _____
4. _____
5. _____

Good Present Situations

1. _____
2. _____
3. _____
4. _____
5. _____

Bad Present Situations

1. _____
2. _____
3. _____
4. _____
5. _____

Emotional Strengths

1. _____
2. _____

3. _____

4. _____

5. _____

Emotional Weaknesses

1. _____

2. _____

3. _____

4. _____

5. _____

Are you willing to take full responsibility for your life—for both the good and the bad? Remember, you may not be at fault for some of the things that have gone wrong. Taking responsibility means celebrating the good things, grieving the losses, and believing that God's plans for you are plans for good, not evil (Jer. 29:11–13).

Facing Your Fears

Before you go to sleep give all your worries to God.
He's going to be up all night anyway.—Anonymous

Fear is a major element in the development of unhealthy relationships because fear and controlling behavior go hand in glove. Hidden within most attempts to control others is an element of fear. Of course, we may not appear to be afraid—that's the beauty of a glove. It insulates the hand within, and it also masks the appearance of what is concealed.

Your controlling behavior may come across as confidence, competence, righteousness, love, concern, "only trying to help," or any number of other "positive attributes." You may even fool yourself with these attitudes because there is genuine good in them. Since they are not what most people would identify as shortcomings, this kind of "good" controlling behavior hides the fear driving it.

Here's an example: a woman is dating a man who is looking for a job. She likes him, but because of her warped view of herself, she assumes that she has to be doing something for him to win his love. She is also afraid that he'll meet someone else. So she decides to "help" him with his job search. Before long his entire career is in her capable hands. The boundaries between business and dating become hopelessly blurred. Even though he takes full advantage of her supposed "no strings attached" help, he feels cramped by her control. Meanwhile, she strongly doubts that he would stay with her as much if she weren't his "assistant." This kind of codependent relationship breeds resentment and burdens a potentially good relationship.

In this example, when did "good" helping cross the line to become controlling behavior? _____

_____

_____

What role did hidden fear play? _____

_____

_____

Cite a situation in your life where fear motivated you to cross the line from helping to controlling behavior. _____

_____

_____

How are your relationships strained by your fear and controlling behavior?

_____

_____

Can you think of a positive behavior that you may be using in a negative way to control someone else? _____

_____

_____

Sometimes you may find yourself obsessing over others when you cannot control them. You may try to imagine what they are doing and thinking, what they meant by what they said. This sort of endless worrying is a sign of unhealthy relationships. One of the best ways to deal with it is to release each person to

UNHEALTHY RELATIONSHIPS

God's care and trust God to take control. List some obsessive worries that you continue to fret about regarding another person:_____

_____

_____

Now take a moment to hand each worry over to God, one by one. If you take them back, hand them over again.

If you are to gain power over codependency, you must face your fears. You must dare to look beneath your "image" to find what you are afraid of because fear triggers controlling behavior. List three things you are afraid of that trigger your controlling behavior:

1. _____

2. _____

3. _____

Create a personal survival plan to cope realistically with each fear. In your imagination, carry the catastrophe all the way through until you have envisioned a way to survive your worst fear in a healthy way. Imagine what you would do to deal with the pain, how you would cope with losses. If applicable, research and plan specific action to care for yourself and minor children if what you fear came to pass. Write out your survival plan for each area of fear._____

_____

_____

_____

Discuss these concerns with your workbook partner and support group. Get phone numbers and names of professionals who are part of your plan.

Establishing Relationship Boundaries

Keep on being brave! It will bring you great rewards.
—Hebrews 10:35 CEV

People sometimes say, "Okay, that's it! This is where I draw the line." Those who are "rescuers," "caretakers," or otherwise codependent usually don't draw the line soon enough or clearly enough. They may not even be sure where it should be drawn.

Establishing relational boundaries involves drawing the line between your life and the lives of others. Gaining power over unhealthy relationships means accepting full responsibility for your life and letting go of responsibility for the lives of others. There are several areas in which you can overstep boundaries into the lives of others or others can cross the line into your life.

Physical life: You overstep others' boundaries whenever you try to control their physical behavior: what they do, how they do it, where they go, when they go, and so on. Certainly, there are appropriate boundaries, especially within marriage, but you cannot control others' responses to the boundaries. You can choose what the consequence will be if the other person's physical actions are unacceptable. Describe one area in which you feel a need to inappropriately control someone's physical behavior. _____

_____

Emotional life: You overstep others' boundaries whenever you try to control, fix, or assume responsibility for how they feel. That includes trying to make them love you, make them happy, or make them sorry for what they have done. Describe one area in which you may have tried to control someone's emotional life. _____

_____

Spiritual life: You overstep others' boundaries whenever you take responsibility for their spiritual lives: playing God in their lives, convicting them of every little sin, dictating God's will for them, or using spiritual manipulations, such as trying to "put the fear of God into them." Describe a time when you may have tried to control someone's spiritual life. _____

_____

Mental and intellectual life: You overstep others' boundaries when you think for them, speak for them, or try to solve their problems instead of allowing them to figure things out for themselves. There is nothing wrong with being supportive, but you violate others' intellectual boundaries whenever you insist that your way is the only right way, give unsolicited advice, and act as if they are accountable to you for whatever they do. Can you think of a time when you have violated someone's mental and intellectual boundaries? _____

_____

_____

Financial life: You overstep others' boundaries when you take responsibility for their financial irresponsibility: allowing them to live in your home without contributing to the household, covering bounced checks, and/or allowing them to continually borrow when they refuse to pay back what has previously been borrowed. This also includes trying to manipulate them by giving them money. Write about a time you may have tried to control someone through finances. _____

_____

Now let's look at the other side of the coin. Are you allowing someone to inappropriately control you? Write a name (or names) next to each statement if it describes how someone in your life tries to control you.

Physical life: Others overstep your boundaries whenever they endanger your physical well-being, threaten to do bodily harm, invade your privacy, or force you to behave physically or sexually in ways that are unacceptable to you.

_____

Emotional life: No one can overstep your emotional boundaries without your involvement. However, some people try to make you feel certain emotions. You also allow others to invade your boundaries when you carry their burdens, feel their feelings instead of holding on to what you feel yourself, or worry over things you have no power to control in their lives._____

_____

Spiritual life: Others overstep your spiritual boundaries whenever they require you to stifle your spiritual life to make them feel more comfortable. They may try to impose certain spiritual "requirements" by speaking for God in your life or imply that you share the guilt of their sins. Whenever you bear the weight of others' spiritual lives or sins, your spiritual boundaries are weak.

_____

Mental and intellectual life: Others cannot make you think in any particular way unless you agree to play mind games with them. However, they encroach on your intellectual life when they try to force you to change your opinion or beliefs, and you may do so in an attempt to be accepted by them. You allow your boundaries to be crossed when you change your mind to appease them, when you are consumed with trying to figure out how to resolve their problems, and when you read books and find yourself thinking more in terms of how the "self-help" helps them instead of you. _____

_____

Financial life: Others overstep your financial boundaries whenever they take away financial security or rely on you to provide more than your fair share in given circumstances. They also cross your boundaries when they violate explicit financial commitments they have made to you, such as not paying back a loan or "borrowing" money without asking (i.e., stealing).

_____

Are you willing to release responsibility for the people whose names you have written beside the statements? If so, sign your initials after each area you are willing to release. Do it whether or not the person accepts responsibility to care for himself or herself.

Make it your goal to stop trespassing in others' lives. Commit yourself to acknowledge every time you overstep boundaries; confess this fault to yourself, your workbook partner and support group, and God. Move in the direction of trespassing less and less.

Decide if you are willing to allow others to continue to trespass in your life. Decide what behavior is unacceptable to you. What are you willing to do about it? At some point communicate what your boundaries are, what you intend to do to protect them, and what you will do if your boundaries are violated.

You may need to confront some people about their tendency to ignore or refuse to honor your boundaries. List anyone in your life with whom you need to discuss a "no trespassing agreement." It doesn't mean ending these relationships (unless they are abusive and intolerable). It means working on these issues and enforcing boundaries openly, honestly, and without manipulation.

_____

_____

_____

_____

Dealing with
the Past

God grant me the serenity to accept the things I cannot change, the courage to change the things I can, and the wisdom to know the difference. Amen.

The behavior of others—behavior that you had no power to control—has deeply affected your life. Although you cannot control others, you can control your attitude and actions in response to their effect on you.

In her best-selling book *Codependent No More*, Melody Beattie says, "A codependent person is one who has let another person's behavior affect him or her, and who is obsessed with controlling that person's behavior." In gaining power over unhealthy relationships, you must learn to recognize where the behavior of others has affected you, whether or not you let it happen; you take ownership of the effects in your life and turn them into something from which new life can grow. That means learning to deal with the effects that have already been dumped into your life in a way that hastens your healing and works to your benefit.

Your obsessive need to control is connected to feelings of powerlessness that arise when you are unable to protect yourself from pain. If you were hurt by others when life was out of your control, you will naturally feel much safer when any part of life is under your control. Your desire for security is understandable, but trying to control everything simply doesn't work. Instead, you need to look back at some of the things that have happened to you in the past and deal positively with the hurts.

One way to do this is to honestly assess how the behavior of others has made you feel powerless in your life. On the following chart, create a catalog of the way others' behavior affected you. Column one is your age when you were hurt. Column two is the name of the person whose behavior affected you. Column three is the description of that person's behavior. Column four describes the way this affected your life. Column five rates your sense of powerlessness on a scale of 1 to 10 (1 means you felt absolutely powerless; 10 means you had sufficient power to stop negative effects on your life).

For example, you might write: age—10–15; who—Mom; what—drunk; what effect—had to take care of siblings/emotional nightmare; power level—1. Don't exclude people who have died; don't try to resolve your feelings. Just make a catalog of each period of time.

Age in Years	Who	What	What Effect	Power Level
0–5	_____	_____	_____	_____
5–10	_____	_____	_____	_____
10–15	_____	_____	_____	_____
15–20	_____	_____	_____	_____
20–30	_____	_____	_____	_____
30–40	_____	_____	_____	_____
40–50	_____	_____	_____	_____
50–60	_____	_____	_____	_____
60+	_____	_____	_____	_____

As you worked on your list, intense feelings may have emerged. Accept your feelings as valid. Acknowledge how you honestly feel, identify where the feelings originated (at which phase of your life), and express your feelings in some tangible, nondestructive way. You may choose to write, talk to a supportive friend, pound your pillow, or cry yourself to sleep. Whatever you honestly feel or don't feel is okay, but you need to express these feelings. What emotions did you have to deal with as you worked on your list? _____

_____

_____

How will you express these feelings? _____

_____

_____

Does this exercise help you understand your need to control **others**? Give one example in which you are behaving in a controlling way because of feelings of powerlessness you experienced in an earlier relationship or situation.

_____

_____

Sorting Out
Obstacles and
Injuries

A place for everything and everything in its place.—Isabella Mary Beeton

There must be some obstacle or injury that causes you to avoid, neglect, or refuse to take responsibility for the parts of your life that are missing. There are reasons you neglected your talents or abandoned your long-lost dreams. The only way you will be able to develop a whole life and healthy relationships is to identify which obstacles and injuries hold you back. Then you can deal with them in a healthy way.

Imagine that your life is represented by a house, and in your house is a closet crammed full of parts of your life that you've been missing. You've been too busy in other rooms, filled with important activities and people who need you, to think about what's in the closet. Besides, you dare not open the door for fear of being overwhelmed.

What things are missing in your life? Recall your talents, treasures, dreams, and avoided issues. You know they are important, but you probably don't know how to sort them all out in a way that will improve your relationships. This next section will help you sort things out.

Don't give in to the temptation to stuff everything back in the closet and close the door again. Instead, you need to categorize each item, learn what to do with each group of items once they are sorted out, and realize that you don't have to deal with all your issues at once. We've included seven boxes you can use to help you sort out your issues. Since you're dealing with human life, not things, a neglected part of your life may be associated with more than one category. If so, put it in all categories where it fits.

1. The Hurt Box

Include anything associated with emotional injury. Whenever you have been wronged, by life or by another person, the experience leaves a painful splinter in your soul. A child with a splinter in her hand will cry, "Don't touch it! It will hurt!" List anything missing from your life that triggers a "Don't touch it!" response when you get close to it: _____

_____

_____

2. The Loss Box

Include anything associated with a loss of any kind: a job, self-respect, freedom, trust, beliefs, money, innocence, possessions, health, friendship, roots, a sense of security, death, or divorce. Loss also involves the things that someone should have done for you and the things that you missed out on. Perhaps your parents neglected your basic needs, and you kept waiting for someone to take care of you as you should have been cared for. You may have left some things undone because you are still waiting for the love that you missed to suddenly appear. These are things you balk at doing for yourself because it feels like closing the door on the possibility of someone, someday, loving you as you should have been loved as a child. List the missing parts of your life that belong in the Loss Box.

_____

_____

_____

3. The Shame Box

Include anything you feel the need to hide or keep secret, anything associated with pretending in order to be accepted, anything you don't do because you feel unworthy or undeserving, anything you consider too expensive even though you have the money, anything you cannot imagine asking help with (out of fear of exposure), anything excluded or not tried because you think something wrong with you disqualifies you, or anything you can't talk about. (See Part 1, "Shame," for further help with this.) List the missing parts of your life that belong in the Shame Box. _____

_____

_____

4. The Fear Box

Include anything that arouses fear: fear of rejection, fear of the consequences, fear of someone else's reaction, fear of abandonment, or fear of letting go of control. What are you missing out on because you are afraid? List the missing parts of your life that belong in the Fear Box. _____

_____

_____

5. The Guilt Box

Include anything associated with guilty feelings: if you feel guilty for not doing it, if you assume you would feel guilt if you did do it, if you feel condemned by others for doing or not doing it. (Part 1, "Shame," may also help you with this.) List the missing parts of your life that belong in the Guilt Box.

_____

_____

6. The "Because of Them" Box

Include anything you do not do because of others, their expectations of you, their dependence on you, or what they might do if you did this. Anything missing from your life associated with blaming others or using them as a reason or excuse for your failure to act goes in this box. What are the missing parts of your life that belong in the Because of Them Box? _____

_____

_____

7. The Practical Box

Include anything you don't do for practical reasons, such as lack of resources, conflicting commitments, and actual limitations based on reality. List the missing parts of your life that belong in the Practical Box: _____

_____

_____

Identifying the things that are missing in your life helps you recognize your injuries and obstacles. As you review the lists you just completed, ask God to give you wisdom about each "missing part" you noted. As you think about your boxes, you may see that some of the items are things you can face, with God's help, starting right now. Some may be things that you cannot or do not want to face at this time. Some may be things that you'll need professional help to deal with.

Beside each item, place a letter *N*—meaning I'll deal with this *now*—or place a letter *L*—meaning I'll deal with this *later*—or place a letter *H*—meaning I'll get *help* from a friend, a support group, or a professional counselor to deal with this.

Now put the boxes away. You can work through the issues one at a time.

Using Your Strength Wisely

What would you give to get back your soul?—Matthew 16:26 CEV

People locked into caretaking or "helping" relationships are usually very strong individuals who need to learn to apply their strength to their personal problems instead of pouring it all into other people's troubles. These strong people may use much of their strength to suppress, deny, or ignore their true feelings.

As you've worked through this part of the book, you've probably begun to see that some things in your life need your attention. Author and speaker Fred Smith has said, "A problem is a problem if I can do something about it. If I cannot do something about it, it is a fact of life." You waste your strength when you try to change a fact of life or try to ignore a real problem. It takes as much strength to actively ignore a problem as it does to solve it. It takes more strength to try to change the facts of life than to face them and learn to live in spite of them.

List three personal problems—things you *can* do something about—you are willing to use your strength to solve:

1. _____
2. _____
3. _____

UNHEALTHY RELATIONSHIPS

List three "facts of life" in your situation—things on which you may have wasted your strength by trying to change what is not in your power to change (these may include loved ones' addictions, conditions, choices, and so on):

1. _____
2. _____
3. _____

List the names of those you are going to "let go" now that you better understand some of the unhealthy ways you may meddle in or try to control the lives of others:

1. _____
2. _____
3. _____

Reward yourself! You've completed Part 2 of your journey toward emotional freedom. Take a moment to write out the three most important lessons you've learned about freedom from unhealthy relationships.

1. _____
2. _____
3. _____

Now do something nice for yourself!

Part 3

Depression

Lately I've felt a lot like crying. Of course I don't want to be a downer, so I'm hiding it as much as possible. But this sadness just won't leave me. I'm exhausted and I don't feel good, and it's hard for me to keep going. For me, the best part of the day is going to sleep at night.—Donna P.

According to the National Depression Screening Day project, depression is an emotional condition characterized by these typical indicators:

- I don't enjoy the things I used to.
- I feel hopeless about the future.
- I feel worthless and not needed.
- I am gaining or losing weight.
- I get tired for no reason.
- I am sleeping too little or too much.
- I feel downhearted, blue, and sad.
- I think about death and even about suicide.*

If you are experiencing any of these symptoms, you will find the following pages helpful and encouraging. You may, however, discover that you need additional help in working through your questions and issues. If so, please seek counsel from a qualified professional by calling 1-800-NEW-LIFE.

Depression surrounds life with darkness, blocking your joy and robbing you of the simple pleasures you should be free to appreciate. Breaking free from depression will dramatically clear the way for your journey into emotional freedom.

*If you are experiencing any suicidal thoughts, find help immediately. Do not continue to work on this book. Set it aside for now, and talk to your pastor or therapist or call 1-800-NEW-LIFE.

Finding Motivation (When You Don't Feel Like Moving)

The more desperately we need God's help, the more aware we are of his power and his presence.—Stephen Arterburn

When you are depressed, the tendency is to draw away from people and the usual interactions of everyday life. Isolation is a major obstacle to overcoming depression because you will need support from someone whose perspective is not clouded to help you see your way clear. That's why, if you are dealing with depression, it's very important for you to work with your workbook companion on this part—even if you haven't been including her or him in the other parts. In fact, in this part, special instructions called "Support Notes" are provided for your workbook partner. It is also helpful to let your support group know if you are depressed.

If you are depressed, you need to know three things:

1. There is hope, even if you can't feel hope right now. You can begin moving in the direction of relief before you feel hopeful.

2. When you're depressed, thinking clearly is difficult. Some symptoms of depression are being unable to concentrate, having clouded thoughts, laboring to keep your mind focused, and feeling overwhelmed by minor decisions that need to be made. These symptoms are experienced intellectually and emotionally but

may be caused by physical conditions affecting your brain chemistry. Your thoughts may be slow in getting through or labored because of real biological causes. Be patient with yourself, and don't give up!

3. You sincerely want to resume a normal life, even if you don't act like it. Many times when you are depressed, you appear unwilling to help yourself, irritable, or uncooperative. Other people may assume you don't sincerely want to find a way out of your darkened mood. This assumption can provoke harsh judgmental reactions, which do nothing to help anyone in the situation. Therefore, this journey will be guided in a nonjudgmental and compassionate way, accepting that you don't want to be miserable. The instructions given to the support person will educate him or her to see beyond your symptoms and respond with compassion.

To keep yourself moving toward any goal, you need to become aware of the benefits you will receive. That is usually as simple as thinking about your goal and imagining what your rewards will be once you reach it. Being relieved of depression will have a dramatic effect on these areas:

- Your inner life
- Your relationships
- Your work

Briefly write your feelings about these possibilities:

When I think about finding relief from my emotional pain, I feel

_____.

When I think about being able to enjoy my life, I feel _____

_____

_____

_____.

DEPRESSION

When I think about improving the lives of my family members, I feel

_____ .

Consider how you could benefit from overcoming depression and being able to enjoy life again. In what ways do you want to experience inner relief from the pain? _____

_____

_____

What relationships with loved ones could be better if you were not depressed?

_____

_____

What relationships at work could be improved? _____

_____

_____

What could be improved in your view of yourself? _____

_____

_____

When you consider the people closest to you, who rely on you to meet needs in their lives, how could you better meet their needs if you weren't depressed?

_____

_____

When was the last time you were really able to enjoy a special time in your life, perhaps a holiday or vacation? _____

_____

_____

Now make a prayer list, asking God to help you with the things you desire to change as you overcome your depression:

1. _____   5. _____
2. _____   6. _____
3. _____   7. _____
4. _____   8. _____

Support Notes

You may be able to see clearly how much better life could be for your friend and be able to envision a hopeful future for her. She may not be able to see that far. It is good to verbalize your hopeful vision for her future as long as you don't insist that she be able to envision it with you. She may be able to see only what is wrong, what is missing, what is upsetting or frustrating. Don't try to make her feel the hope you feel for her at this point. Just help her turn her list of negatives around to be a list of positive reasons to overcome whatever is causing the darkened moods.

For example, if she says, "I hate myself," the item on the list of benefits would be to accept myself as being valuable. If she says, "I can't function at work; I hate my job, but I'm afraid I'm going to be fired," the item on the list would be to succeed at work and have greater security in my career.

Once the list of negatives is turned around into positive benefits, read the list to her and encourage her so that she can receive these benefits. If both of you feel comfortable praying together, offer to pray for these benefits to be realized in her life.

Your Path Will Be Unique

Wise people have enough sense to find their way.—Proverbs 14:8 CEV

Although depression can be caused in several ways, the symptoms are similar. Please place a check mark beside any of the following statements that apply to you:

___ You feel low.
___ You lose interest or pleasure in what you used to enjoy.
___ You have depressed moods even when your circumstances are good.
___ There has been a marked shift in your behavior.
___ You cry easily.
___ You lack motivation and you don't care anymore.
___ You have trouble sleeping, or you sleep all the time.
___ You have lost your appetite.
___ You lack interest in sex.
___ You are often fatigued.
___ You have general thoughts of death or suicide.
___ You are unable to concentrate, and thought processes seem slowed.
___ You feel overwhelmed by simple decisions.
___ You are pessimistic.
___ Your feelings of guilt are intense (whether or not they are legitimate).

___ You struggle with low self-esteem, feeling worthless, unwanted, unloved, dirty, or sinful.

___ You can't function well with others in social situations and at work.

___ You lose your motivation to care for personal needs such as eating, grooming, personal hygiene, and so on.

___ You are irritable, overreacting to little problems.

___ You are beset by physical discomforts and maybe even chronic pain, which may be quite severe.

Most people have experienced some form of depression. They recall experiencing these kinds of feelings, and they have a theory about what caused them and how they were able to get out of their bout of depression. Their theory about the cause and cure of their bout with the blues will reflect their general focus in life. A medical doctor may focus more on the possible physical factors; a pastor, priest, or other spiritual adviser may focus on the spiritual influences; a counselor or psychologist may focus on the relational or psychological roots of depression; someone who has experienced the power of positive thinking may see depression primarily in terms of having a negative mind-set. In actual fact, you are a whole person: body, mind, and spirit. You need to consider all areas of your being as possible contributors to depression.

Are you willing to accept that there may be influences in the following areas of life that contribute to your depression? Please circle Y (=Yes) or N (=No) after each phrase, indicating whether you think it could possibly apply to you (keep an open mind!):

Physical/biological conditions Y/N

Emotional/psychological conditions Y/N

Spiritual influences Y/N

Mental/intellectual influences Y/N

Relational or experiential influences Y/N

Support Notes

You probably have your own theories that can be a helpful part of understanding the unique factors contributing to your friend's depression. You can include them in the discussion; however, please don't try to persuade her to accept your perspective. Your job is to help her gather as complete a picture as possible. Your objectivity is needed at this point.

During this phase, it is more important to ask questions to help her uncover what might be important pieces of the puzzle rather than to tell her what you think. Remember, she has more access to the answers for the problem than you do.

Dealing with Your Addictions

We are wise to reevaluate our priorities before a crisis forces us to do so.
—Stephen Arterburn

Y**ou** cannot overcome depression while relying on addictive-compulsive behavior to alter your mood, especially if you are using drugs and/or alcohol, which are depressants. Depression and addiction feed on each another. Being in bondage to some form of addiction will have a dramatic impact on your ability to identify the source of your depression. You need to deal with your addictive-compulsive behavior and depression simultaneously. If you deaden the pain with an addiction, you distract yourself momentarily, but you do nothing to identify and deal with the source of your pain. When you use an addiction to mask the pain, you lose touch with your sense of what is really hurting and what needs attention. In this way your use of an addiction can keep you in depression because it covers the real source of your pain.

You may not feel comfortable telling your support person the exact nature of your addictive-compulsive behavior. You don't have to. What is important is that you acknowledge addictive-compulsive behavior and decide to get appropriate help.

What do you do to temporarily alter your mood when you are feeling pain associated with depression? _____

What substances or experiences do you use to escape the pain of living your life? Place a check mark next to any addictions you have used at any time in the past. Circle any of these addictive-compulsive behaviors you currently use (within the last six months).

__ Alcohol

__ Marijuana

__ Narcotics

__ Sex addiction (including the use of pornography or any form of sexual stimulation)

__ Relational/romance addiction

__ Compulsive gambling

__ Compulsive overeating

__ Compulsive spending

__ Codependency (losing yourself in the needs of others)

__ Workaholism

__ Religious addiction

__ Other _____

Are you overwhelmed by the thought of trying to face life without your addiction to help you cope? Consider whether an inpatient treatment program would enable you to break the cycle. Call an inpatient treatment program, and talk to a staff person about the program and how it might work for you. (There is no obligation, and the call can be anonymous.)

Do something today to seek treatment for your addictive or compulsive behavior. Call a treatment program; attend a support group or a twelve-step group; tell your support person that you realize you may have an addiction to deal with; make an appointment with a counselor who specializes in helping persons with your particular addiction.

Support Notes

If the person is willing to acknowledge addictive-compulsive behavior, help him take the steps necessary to get on the road to recovery. Denial is a powerful deterrent. If you see that he is ignoring a problem with addiction, speak honestly about what you see. If he feels uncomfortable reaching out for help but is willing to receive it, you make the calls and arrange for him to speak with someone in an appropriate treatment program. It may take time to research and locate treatment that fits with his values, schedule, and financial considerations. His willingness to accept treatment is a major effort on his part. Your part is to make the practical arrangements to get him into the treatment program he needs.

The Progression Out of the Pit

Don't be afraid. I have rescued you. I have called you by name; now you belong to me.—Isaiah 43:1 CEV

It is encouraging to know that your depression may clear up by your taking care of yourself—body, mind, and spirit—and nurturing primary relationships. You will be able to recognize that your depression is related to something more than depletion of a basic need if the condition isn't resolved by nourishing yourself.

Starting today, do the following to improve your basic health:

- Take a multivitamin/mineral supplement.
- Eat nourishing foods from the basic food groups during your meals. You may also want to use a diet supplement or healthful drink to give you the nourishment your body needs if your depression has caused you to lose your appetite.
- Take a daily walk or exercise at least twenty minutes a day. (It has been proven that physical exercise can raise your spirits by increasing the level of endorphins, brain chemicals that act as natural pain relievers. Whenever you exercise vigorously, your body releases endorphins, which can help you feel better emotionally. You may not feel like exercising when you start out, but once you choose to

exercise, you unleash a natural high that can help you overcome your darkened mood.

- Get enough rest. Arrange your schedule to allow sufficient sleep each night. (Don't become dependent on sleep-inducing medication or narcotics. Also cutting back on caffeine can promote better rest for your body.)

Write your honest responses to the following questions:

Are you willing to make these basic changes in your daily life? Explain.

_____

_____

Will you accept necessary help from your support person to change your schedule, eating habits, and daily routine? Explain. _____

_____

_____

What kind of exercise do you most enjoy? _____

_____

Are you willing to exercise vigorously to help yourself feel better? Explain.

_____

_____

Do you feel unable to do vigorous exercise? What conditions make you feel unable? Is there any form of exercise you could do, given the conditions you must deal with? _____

_____

_____

What practical obstacles seem to be in your way that you would need to over-come to begin basic self-care today? _____

_____

_____

Support Notes

Making any kind of change from a normal routine takes practice, even when you are not depressed. For the person who is depressed, these simple changes may seem overwhelming. You may need to take charge and provide these changes for your loved one. If you can, take the walk with her. You may even need to get her up and going. Use the time to talk about the day's journey. Be patient with her feelings but insist that she take these steps that will help her.

Encourage her to tell you any obstacles she sees that would keep her from making these changes. Then take it upon yourself to eliminate the obstacles for her.

Taking Care of Your Physical Health

I am the LORD your God, and I cure your diseases.—Exodus 15:26 CEV

Depression is experienced as an emotional condition, but it is often related to physical conditions, routines, and behaviors. Depression can be caused by the following:

- Diabetes and hypoglycemia
- Some medications, such as ones used to lower high blood pressure
- Imbalances in the endocrine system
- Premenstrual syndrome (PMS) or menopause
- Postpartum blues, hysterectomy, or miscarriage
- Brain injuries

Getting a physical checkup from a medical doctor will ensure that your physical health problems are being treated and will let you know if your depression may be caused partially by a medical problem.

When did you last have a complete physical examination? _____

_____

_____

_____

If you have not had one since you began to experience depression, will you schedule one today? Explain. _____

_____

_____

Are you aware of any health conditions that are not being treated?

_____

_____

Can you think of any physical changes or health conditions that might contribute to depression? _____

_____

Are you willing to take care of your physical health? Explain.

_____

_____

Depression can cause you to lose all interest in personal grooming. But neglecting your personal grooming can also make you feel down. Taking care of your physical appearance may seem like a chore, but it is an effort that will help you feel better (unless you are dealing with a depressive illness that has physical or biochemical causes). When you clean up and dress up, your spirits usually go up. Sometimes taking a shower, applying makeup, cologne, or perfume, putting on new clothes, and getting a haircut or new hairstyle may help you to have a brighter outlook on life as well.

Do you think you are depressed because of your physical condition and appearance, or are you neglecting your physical condition and appearance because you are depressed? _____

_____

_____

Are you willing to clean up and dress up in an attempt to feel better? Explain.

_____

_____

_____

_____

Support Notes

Whatever the cause of the depression, your friend probably won't be enthusiastic about doing these action steps. You can help by making the appointment for the medical evaluation and offering to take him to the appointment. Once he has medical confirmation that his physical condition will allow him to exercise, you can encourage him by offering to exercise with him or by helping him make arrangements for an exercise program he enjoys.

Do what you can to encourage him to care for his physical appearance without being critical of how he looks. He probably is struggling with low self-esteem and will not respond positively to criticism as an attempt to motivate him. Some conditions may make it very difficult to maintain even the most basic grooming routine. If he is dealing with a season of intense grief, perhaps it is not important for him to dress up. The somber dress may be a valid expression of grief. If his depression is caused by a physical condition, he could look his best every day, and it wouldn't make him feel better emotionally. Help him do what he can, note what helps and what does not, then keep these things in mind when he begins to define the contributing factors to his depression.

Nurturing a Healthy Mind

You are where you are, you are what you are because of what has gone into your mind. You can change where you are, you can change what you are by changing what goes into your mind.—Zig Ziglar

There are probably things on your mind weighing you down. You may face stressful situations or problems demanding your attention. You may be grappling with losses while trying to establish a new way of life without whatever or whoever you have lost. You may have worries and fears that overshadow all other thoughts.

You can easily get depressed if you carry a burden on your mind without moving toward resolving it, for example,

- worrying over things that are not in your power to change.
- worrying over problems that might arise but do not yet exist.
- worrying over someone else's life and carrying that person's burden.
- mulling over a problem, yet not taking action to resolve it.

List the things on your mind that are weighing you down:

1. _____
2. _____
3. _____
4. _____

5. _____
6. _____

For each item, answer these two questions:

1. Is this problem your responsibility, or is it someone else's problem? If it is yours, mark *M* (for mine) next to the item; if not, mark *S* (for someone else's).

2. Is this problem in your power to change? If it is, mark *Y* next to the item; if not, mark *N*.

Circle the items on your list that have both an *M* and a *Y*. These are your problems.

Draw a line through every item that either is not your problem or is not within your power to change. As you cross it off your list, try to mentally unload it from the burden you carry on your mind.

Discuss each circled item (your responsibility and within your power to change) with your workbook companion. Decide what you can do to try to resolve the problem or to get help to resolve the problem.

Besides the worries and problems you carry around in your mind, your feelings can be powerfully influenced by what you choose to put into your mind. What are you feeding your mind through what you see, hear, read, and think about? You have the power and responsibility to choose what you feed your mind. Consider these negative sources, and check the ones that you expose yourself to:

___ Soap operas
___ Pornography
___ Conversations with negative people
___ Music with depressing or vulgar lyrics
___ Entertainment filled with violence or centered on fatalistic themes
___ Negative religion

__ Romance novels
__ Horror/crime novels

Of the things that feed your thoughts regularly, what negative influences do you see? _____

_____

_____

What positive influences? _____

_____

_____

Are you willing to adapt your mental diet to exclude the negative and increase the positive? _____

_____

_____

Support Notes

As your friend lists what weighs on her mind, it can be a healing experience for you to validate that her concerns matter. Feel free to sympathize and affirm your sorrow that she is hurting deeply. Concentrate on listening carefully to her words and her emotions. However, it is important not to get so caught up in the emotion that you lose the ability to help her list her problems and burdens. She needs your help to unravel the jumble of emotions and issues into a list of separate problems. You will also help her see whether the burden is hers to bear and whether it is in her power to change. Don't get into an argument over this. If she insists that something is in her power to change, go ahead and decide what she can do to change it. At this point she may realize that it is not in her power to change, even though she wishes that it were.

Nourishing Your Spiritual Health

Spiritual strength can uphold you when it seems that all other strength is spent.—Stephen Arterburn

When you've got the blues, the invading darkness can reach to the depths of your being, even casting shadows over your spiritual life. Many ways to nourish yourself spiritually can offset some of the stress and anxiety associated with depression. Doing things that lift your spirits is a healthy part of an overall plan to develop emotional health.

Here are some ways to nourish your spiritual health:

Pray. Prayer can take many therapeutic forms. Even if you are not sure about your relationship with God, you can still benefit from prayer.

Are you willing to pray? Why? _____

_____

_____

Pour out your sorrows to God. The Bible says that God collects our tears in a bottle (Ps. 56:8). You are invited to cast your cares upon God because he cares for you. Assume that God cares deeply about you, and pour out your heart before him.

Do you believe that God cares about your sorrows? _____

_____

DEPRESSION

In the Bible, God declares, "I will comfort them and turn their sorrow into happiness" (Jer. 31:13 CEV). Write out how that Scripture could apply to you.

_____

_____

_____

Give thanks. Even though you are troubled, there must be some things in life that you can be thankful for. Expressing thanks to God can elevate your perspective and lighten your mood.

List ten things for which you are grateful:

1. _____   6. _____

2. _____   7. _____

3. _____   8. _____

4. _____   9. _____

5. _____   10. _____

Ask God for the specific things you need, including insight into what is causing your depression, resources to help you, and the ability to enjoy life again. The apostle Paul wrote, "And it is he who will supply all your needs from his riches in glory, because of what Christ Jesus has done for us" (Phil. 4:19 TLB).

How could that Scripture apply to you? _____

_____

_____

_____

List ten needs you would like to ask God to supply:

1. _____   6. _____
2. _____   7. _____
3. _____   8. _____
4. _____   9. _____
5. _____   10. _____

Surround yourself with beauty. Beauty, especially the beauty of nature, can be tremendously refreshing. Take time to relax amid whatever natural beauty is available to you. Walking in the woods, strolling through a field of wildflowers, or sitting on the beach while watching the waves can nourish your spirit. Beauty can also be found in creative works of music and art. Expose yourself to what you find beautiful. Brighten up your surroundings with beautiful colors.

Where do you have access to the beauty of nature? _____
_____
_____

When is the next time you have available you could plan to get out into the beauty of nature? _____
_____
_____

Meditate on things that are true and good. When you are battling depression, you may have the tendency to focus on all that is wrong with the world. Instead, try taking a few moments each day to quiet yourself, relax, and focus your mind on something that is right. Don't get involved in any type of meditation that empties your mind of all focused thought. When you are in a darkened mood, that kind of open-mindedness can lead you farther into darkness.

A beautiful scriptural passage tells us, "Fix your thoughts on what is true and good and right. Think about things that are pure and lovely, and dwell on the fine, good things in others. Think about all you can praise God for and be glad about" (Phil. 4:8 TLB). Why do you think this Scripture could be helpful to you?_____

_____

_____

List some things that are "true, good, or right" that you could meditate on in a quiet moment (think of positive quotes, good facts about your life, Bible verses, and so on):

1. _____   6._____
2. _____   7._____
3. _____   8._____
4. _____   9._____
5. _____   10._____

Be creative in the use of your talents. Use whatever gift of creative expression you have. If you sing, sing out your blues. If you draw or paint, use that medium to express yourself. If you have mechanical ability, be constructive and build something. If you write, compose a poem or song to express your feelings. Creative expression can vent deep emotions that you may not be able to get out any other way. You can also give yourself a sense of accomplishment.

What form of creative expression do you most enjoy? _____

_____

_____

Are you enjoying it now? Explain. _____

_____

_____

Support Notes

Spiritual issues can be a minefield when someone is depressed. Your friend may doubt the existence of God or at least doubt the goodness of any God who would leave him in such despair. When someone is depressed, he often feels exceedingly sinful or guilt-ridden and assumes that God would not receive his prayers. He may also vent his hostilities at God.

You need to be compassionate and allow your loved one to be honest about how he feels regarding spiritual issues, even if that offends your spiritual sensibilities. Now is not the time to point out where he falls short in his spiritual life. If you have a deep relationship with God that you wish he could share, then use your private time of prayer to seek God's help on his behalf rather than try to preach to him right now.

Remind him that his depression also colors his perspective regarding spiritual issues, and his spiritual life may not be as bleak as it seems. Encourage him to do whatever he can to nourish himself spiritually. Perhaps you can offer him whatever access you have to things that can bring beauty and light into his dark world.

Strengthening Relationships That Lift You Up

Friends are gifts we give ourselves.—Anonymous

Human relationships, especially ones within the family, have a forceful impact on your life. Some relationships tear you down, and others build you up. When you're depressed, you need to strengthen relationships that build you up. These are the relationships from which you will draw hope, courage, strength, and support when you are down and while you move back to health. You need to nurture these uplifting relationships because they will be vital to your recovery.

On the other hand, relationships that have power to tear you down may be a significant clue to your depression:

- There are relationships within family systems that can leave you feeling trapped, locked into certain roles or situations that overwhelm you.
- There are love-hate relationships that constantly stir up conflicting emotions.
- There are abusive relationships where you are being abused or being

abusive that evoke deep feelings of shame and degradation without much hope of breaking the destructive cycle.

Any relationship that is destructive or degrading to your human dignity or that of the other person but seems impossible to break free of can lead to depression. (Please see Part 2, "Unhealthy Relationships," for further help with this problem.)

Take care to nurture uplifting relationships so that the other persons will continue to lend you support over the course of time. Be sure to show your appreciation. By respecting these important relationships, you will also gain respect for yourself. Even in your state of depression, you can do some basic things to nurture these relationships rather than exhaust the support they offer.

As you reflect on your relationships, fill in names under each heading. Start with your immediate family, extended family, friends, work associates, support network, and others. Keep going until you have at least five people in the uplifting column.

People Who Lift You Up	People Who Tear You Down
1. _____	1. _____
2. _____	2. _____
3. _____	3. _____
4. _____	4. _____
5. _____	5. _____

Focus your attention on your relationships with these five people as you read over the following list of ways you can strengthen these relationships. After you read each item, write how you will act to strengthen your relationship with each uplifting person in that particular way.

1. Don't label a person in a supportive relationship as your savior. If you see one person as being the only one who can rescue you, the person will naturally draw

away from such an overwhelming burden. Instead of assigning someone the role of savior, accept whatever role the individual can realistically play as part of your support network._____

_____

_____

_____

2. Be willing to face your problems and do whatever you can to help yourself. When you are willing to do as much as you can to help yourself, even if that is severely limited by the symptoms of your depression, others will be more willing to do whatever they can to help you too. _____

_____

_____

3. Express your appreciation and gratitude. Don't assume that because you are depressed and feel desperately needy, people should be obligated to go out of their way to take care of you. If people give of themselves, let them know you appreciate their time, effort, involvement, and whatever else they give you. Remember to say thank you for what they try to do to help you, even if it doesn't make your pain go away. _____

_____

_____

4. Let people know whenever they have a positive impact on your life. They may not be able to see how they are affecting you from your countenance alone.

_____

_____

5. Respect their limitations and boundaries. Don't expect them to give more than they are able of their time, finances, emotions, or anything else. Healthy

people have boundaries they set in relationships and lifestyle that keep them balanced and nourished._____

_____

_____

Now look at the list of people who tear you down. What do you believe you should do about your relationships with them? _____

_____

Please keep three things in mind:

1. You should talk over these difficult relationships with your support person, your support network, and possibly even a counselor if these people are having a serious impact on your life.

2. Before you make any decisions about terminating relationships, seek counsel from your friends, trustworthy family members, counselor, pastor, and any others whose wisdom you value. Sometimes depressed people are tempted to make dramatic decisions in order to "change" things. These are not always wise decisions, so please get wise advice.

3. Part 2, "Unhealthy Relationships," may be helpful to you. However, please complete this part first, then go back if you need to.

Support Notes

This type of evaluation can become the basis for self-condemnation instead of a step toward improving relationships. When someone is depressed, she may become so focused on what she is doing wrong that she loses sight of what she can do to change. Your role is to help her focus on making positive changes rather than condemn herself for not being the world's best friend. Remind her that she may be dealing with an illness that makes her unable to relate as well as she would like. Also remind her that she is loved by those who uplift her and she will not always be as needy as she is now.

DEPRESSION

She may also get sidetracked into focusing on destructive relationships. Unless you are a licensed therapist, you are not equipped to unravel the destructive cords of her relational life. Don't let her get off track from this assignment. Instead, help her focus on looking for the relationships that can have a positive impact. If she cannot identify individuals who are uplifting, try to help her in the process by suggesting people you see as willing to be of help if they were allowed. Include professionals who would be a part of the support network (counselors, support group leaders, doctors, etc.).

Are You Dealing with Normal Depression?

I may walk through valleys as dark as death,
but I won't be afraid.
You are with me.—Psalm 23:4 CEV

As you work through the next few pages, you will learn about the various kinds of depression and the differences between them. Learning this will help you narrow your focus to find the help appropriate for you. You are probably familiar with what is called normal depression.

Normal depression is the typical response of people to overwhelming stress or loss. This type of depression is directly related to identifiable sources of stress. Sometimes normal depression lasts only a short time after a particularly stressful event and may be fairly mild. But it can also linger for longer seasons of time and be severe enough to warrant hospitalization, especially if a person becomes suicidal.

Normal depression is linked to the grieving process you must go through when you experience loss or disappointment. A season of depression during grieving is actually healthy, even though you are experiencing deep sorrow and anguish. If you move through the grief process without getting stuck, you will eventually come out of the depression and resume a normal life. If you get stuck somewhere in grief and stop moving out of loss, depression may overwhelm you. Please circle Y (=Yes) or N (=No) after each of the following questions:

DEPRESSION

In the past year, have you experienced a death (even that of a beloved pet)? Y/N

Have you been through a divorce? Y/N

Have you lost your job? Y/N

Have you lost a close friend for any reason? Y/N

Have you suffered financial loss? Y/N

Have you lost your sense of direction in life? Y/N

Have you lost trust or innocence? Y/N

Have you lost an addiction? Y/N

Have you experienced any other loss? Y/N Explain. _____

_____

_____

Normal depression can also come from being stressed out. Any change in life—good or bad—will create stress. You can experience stress-related depression after completing a major life goal or being fired from your job. When your level of stress is high, it takes its toll on your body, mind, and emotions. Living with a high stress level over a prolonged period of time can lead to depression and exhaustion.

Read this list of stress factors, and mark any that have happened to you in the last year. This list is not comprehensive; it is given to spark your thinking. Add to this list any other stresses that add to your overall level of stress.

___ Death of a spouse

___ Death of immediate family member

___ Divorce or separation in your marriage

___ Divorce or separation of parents

___ Move to a new location

___ Addition to your family

___ Family member moved away from home

___ Completed major goal (such as graduation)

__ Loss of job
__ New job
__ Financial difficulties
__ Purchase or sale of a home
__ Miscarriage or abortion
__ Birth of a baby
__ Long work hours
__ Pressures and deadlines you are racing to meet
__ Other: _____
__ Other: _____

After considering this information, rate your overall stress level on a scale of 1 to 10 (1 means that you don't feel stressed at all; 5 means that you have a moderate level of stress; and 10 means that you feel ready to explode). Write the number here: _____

Normal depression can be the body's way of shutting down so you can deal with stress. Although it is painful, it is a part of the normal process of growing, adapting, and changing that will help you go forward with life.

When your depression is the normal response to an overwhelming loss or stress, you deal with it differently from other forms of depression. A slogan used by Alcoholics Anonymous is an excellent guideline when trying to get out of normal depression. It says, "The only way out is through." You may need to go through your season of grief to get over your depression in a healthy way. Here are some ideas on ways you can help yourself through this process:

- Give yourself some time, but use it well. It has been said that time heals all wounds. That is true only if you use the time to treat whatever wounds you have. If you neglect a wound, whether physical, emotional, or spiritual, it may get infected and grow worse over time. Use this time of pain to tend to the emotional and spiritual wounds you feel.

- Identify where you hurt, why you think you hurt, and get appropriate help.

- Acknowledge the pain of what has happened to you. In our society pretending to be happy when you are not is seen as a virtue. We teach children to be "brave" and not cry over their hurts and losses. We admire the widow or widower who doesn't "fall apart" at the funeral. You might have learned that sorrow is not socially acceptable, and you have adopted the habit of trying to disavow what has happened to you. You may pretend you are fine when you are not.

- Allow yourself to grieve. There are steps in grieving a loss that will help you move beyond loss and back into a life you can enjoy. If you need to know more about grieving, go to the library and read about this very important process, or speak with a grief counselor.

- Itemize and value your losses (rather than compare them to losses of others, which tends to negate their importance). Don't minimize your losses just because they don't seem to be as severe as someone else's.

- Share your pain with someone who understands. Find family members, talk to your workbook companion, or ask your support group to share your loss and sympathize with you in your time of grief.

- Identify major stress factors, and take action to reduce stress as much as possible. Once you have recognized where the stress is coming from in your life, you can make choices to reduce the overall stress level.

- Seek counseling or inpatient treatment if you feel overwhelmed. Just because your depression comes from understandable sources does not mean that you should have to handle it on your own. If you don't feel able to manage life during this season, seek help to put your life in perspective and gain the strength to go on.

How are you using this time of sorrow to treat your emotional and spiritual wounds? _____

_____

_____

Are you growing better or worse with the passage of time? (If you are growing worse, you need to take action to identify and treat your wounds.)

_____

Are you acknowledging the reality of what has happened to you and how you honestly feel, or are you trying to pretend everything is fine?

_____

_____

Do you respect the value of each loss that is important to you, or do you minimize your losses by comparing them to others'? _____

_____

With whom can you share your pain and sorrows? _____

_____

What are you doing to reduce stress in your life? What more can you do?

_____

_____

Do you think you might need professional help to get you through this season?

_____

Support Notes

The purpose of this exercise is to determine if there are some identifiable stresses that would normally cause your loved one to experience some level of depression. You are not supposed to help her work through her loss, nor is it your job to tell her how to reduce her level of stress. The goal is to help her see if her depression may be related to normal depression caused by identifiable stresses. If she seems to need to talk about her losses and the associated pain, move through the questions quickly and then spend time listening to her. If there is a high level of stress in her life, she may be relieved to realize that any-one who had been through her recent experiences would have cause to be depressed.

Are You Dealing with a Depressive Illness?

If your depression has a medical cause, you will find great relief by getting medical care.—Stephen Arterburn

Does your depression occur whether your circumstances are good or bad?

_____

Is there a history of depression or manic depression in your family? Explain.

_____

_____

Are you certain (having had a physical examination by a doctor) that you do not have another disease that may have depression as a secondary condition? Explain. _____

_____

_____

Have you had any head or brain injury that occurred before the onset of depression? _____

_____

What medications and mood-altering substances are you using?

_____

DEPRESSION

Quite often, depression is caused by a physical condition: a chemical imbalance in the brain, a hormonal imbalance, a secondary symptom of disease, a brain injury, or a substance in the body (such as medication or alcohol). For the purposes of this workbook, these forms of depression, caused primarily by physical conditions, will be called depressive illness.

In a booklet prepared by Merrell Dow Pharmaceuticals, Inc., Joseph Talley, M.D., and Beverly Mead, M.D., call depression "a common illness, one of the most common in all of medicine." They explain that many misconceptions regarding depression are commonly held, saying, "We used to think that unusual depression was due to some hidden unhappiness or conflict in a person's life. We now know that many otherwise healthy people who have no reason to be unhappy become depressed, too."

Keeping these possibilities in mind is important because depression that seems unrelated to your circumstances or stress level may be a helpful indicator leading to the discovery of a medical condition that requires treatment. If your depression is one of the rare cases where it is a secondary symptom of disease, you would do well to consider this possibility to spare yourself the frustration, time, and effort of trying to figure out why you are so depressed.

- Both major depression and manic depression can be associated with chemical imbalances in the brain.
- Several forms of hormonal imbalance can have emotional symptoms associated with depression. They include thyroid conditions and conditions related to the endocrine system.
- Hormonal fluctuations experienced during the female menstrual and reproductive cycle often cause depression. Serious depression is reported by up to 30 percent of women several days to a week before and/or just after the start of menstruation. In times past, the condition was largely dismissed as being purely emotional or imaginary. In recent years the condition we know as PMS (premenstrual

syndrome) has been legitimized and successfully treated medically as well as with the use of exercise. Also, it is common to experience depressive illness related to hormonal imbalance at menarche (when a girl first begins menstruating), during menopause, after a miscarriage, after the birth of a child, or after an abortion or a tubal ligation. In these cases the symptoms of depression are caused by fluctuations in the hormonal balance between the ovarian hormones, estrogen and progesterone.

• Drugs that block the release of these hormones have proven to relieve depression and other related physical discomforts. However, using contraceptive pills may cause depression in some women because of the way they affect the hormonal balance.

• Depression can result from a brain injury. If there is physical injury to the brain, it can affect whatever brain functions are conducted by the injured area: emotional perceptions, memory, and thought processes.

• Substances such as alcohol and many other recreational drugs act as depressants in the body. Prescription drugs can also have depression as a possible side effect, which has been seen to be the case with medication routinely used to reduce high blood pressure. If you are taking any type of medication or recreational drug, particularly if you are addicted to alcohol, your depression may be one of the side effects. It can be a deadly combination. There is a high correlation to the incidence of suicide in people who are depressed and addicted to alcohol.

Here are some symptoms and factors associated with depressive illness. Circle Y or N to note whether it applies to you. If you do not know the answer for sure, put a question mark over the Y/N.

1. You experience lowered moods unrelated to whether circumstances are good or bad. Y/N

DEPRESSION

2. You experience sleep disturbances. Y/N

3. You have a family history of depression (symptoms of depression have been seen in parents, grandparents, siblings, aunts, or uncles). Y/N

4. You have significant mood swings from extreme highs to extreme lows that are unrelated to whether circumstances are good or bad. Y/N

If you answered yes to any of the preceding, there is the possibility you are dealing with a chemical imbalance in the brain that may cause your depression. The following are associated with hormonal imbalance that can cause depression:

1. You are at a place in your menstrual cycle where you typically experience depression. Y/N

2. You have recently experienced a miscarriage, an abortion, or a tubal ligation. Y/N

3. You are going through menopause. Y/N

4. You are using a prescription contraceptive that may cause depression as a side effect. Y/N

5. You have a thyroid condition that is not being treated properly. Y/N

If you answered yes to any of the preceding, you may have a hormonal imbalance. The following are medical or pharmaceutical influences associated with depression:

1. You have diabetes, hypoglycemia, or another medical condition known to cause depression in some people. Y/N

2. You have had a head injury, which coincides with the onset of your depression. Y/N

3. You use alcohol. Y/N

4. You use marijuana and/or other recreational drugs. Y/N

5. You use prescription medication that can cause depression as a side effect in some people. Y/N

Enlist the help of your support person to find the information you need to turn your question marks into definite "yes" or "no" statements.

Support Notes

Don't let your friend guess or make assumptions in responding to these statements. If he is not absolutely sure, encourage him to use the question mark. Then help him get the information necessary to find a definite answer. You may even need to do the research for him.

The following information may help you better deal with your friend's depression:

- A chemical imbalance in the brain is caused by a depletion or deficiency of neurotransmitters (the chemicals that transmit messages between nerve endings in the brain). This condition is easily treatable using antidepressant medication, which has been widely used in recent years with much success. A physician must make the determination and administer the treatment. You may want to suggest counseling as well to help your friend learn to adjust to a new way of life.
- If you suspect that your friend may be dealing with a hormonal imbalance of some kind, relief is available. For conditions related to the menstrual cycle, women can seek treatment for PMS and get medical care to help them through times when their estrogen-progesterone levels are fluctuating. A doctor may suggest hormone therapy, an exercise program, or natural progesterone therapy.
- If you think your friend's depression may be related to another disease or be a side effect of some form of medication, discuss this

situation with a doctor and see if there is anything that can allow your friend to medically treat the disease and remain free of depression.

- If your friend is using recreational drugs that may act as depressants, she needs to find a way to stop using them in order to be free from depression. Your friend may be afraid of becoming more depressed and not being able to face life without the help of a substance. Actually, dependence on alcohol, marijuana, or other recreational drugs may be a form of self-medication to deal with undiagnosed and untreated depressive illness. The problem is that self-medication has temporary effects and life-damaging consequences. If your friend has not yet sought treatment for any addiction, consider suggesting it in conjunction with getting medical treatment for possible clinical depression. You may find that once the depression is treated, she will not have the same compulsive need for self-medication.

When someone may be dealing with a form of depressive illness, you cannot wait until he "feels like it" to get medical treatment. Do whatever you can to identify what is causing him to hesitate. Take whatever steps are necessary to get him a professional evaluation from a doctor who has a successful track record helping people with depressive illness.

Are You Dealing with Negative Attitudes and Beliefs?

You harvest what you plant, whether good or bad.—Proverbs 14:14 CEV

How do you see your attitudes and beliefs relating to your depression?

_____

_____

Have you ever experienced a change in attitude or belief that affected your life in a positive way? What happened? _____

_____

_____

Would you be willing to take steps to change your attitudes and beliefs if you knew that would help you break free of depression? Explain.

_____

_____

Some depression is brought on by years of living with negative attitudes and self-destructive beliefs. Apart from depressive illness, to a large degree, your level of happiness is a choice you make. Negative attitudes and faulty beliefs alone are enough to depress you. If they are added to other contributing factors, they can magnify the problems considerably. The good news is that you can change your attitudes and beliefs and, in so doing, change your level of happiness.

The first step in correcting any problem is to identify it and admit that it exists. In this section, you will look at some negative attitudes and beliefs that can contribute to depression. You may also think of others particular to you that you want to add.

Remember, the purpose in identifying them is not to condemn yourself. The purpose is to make corrections that can lead to relief.

Rate yourself on a scale of 1 to 10 on how much you hold these attitudes and beliefs that can contribute to depression (1 means you never hold this attitude or belief; 5 means you have this attitude or belief sometimes; and 10 means you hold it most or all of the time). List any other negative attitudes you see that may contribute to your depression, and rate yourself on them too.

If you are willing to have a gauge of whether you perceive yourself as others perceive you, ask your support person to rate you on each one in the same way. If you don't want the person's perspective, you don't have to do this. If you do want the input, go over your ratings together and compare. You can choose to change your rating if you like after comparing the two perspectives.

Rate yourself on the following:

Statement	Rating
"The world owes me!"	_____
"It's their fault!"	_____
"I can make it on my own."	_____
"If only . . ."	_____
"I deserve to be miserable."	_____
"I can never forgive them (or myself)."	_____
"I'll never have enough."	_____

"I am powerless." _____

_____ _____

_____ _____

List the three statements that received the highest ratings:

1. _____
2. _____
3. _____

Read these explanations of the statements, and try to answer the question(s) following each of the three that apply to you:

"The world owes me!" If you have been deprived, hurt, or abused, you may have the attitude the world owes you or particular people owe you. This attitude leads to failure to accept responsibility for your recovery, conflict in relationships, lowered productivity, and resentment. We live in a broken world where life isn't fair. No one will ever be able to make up to you precisely what you feel is owed. The only way for these emotionally weighty debts to be reduced is for you to cancel them with forgiveness.

What deprivation, hurt, or abuse caused you to feel that the world owes you?

_____

_____

Are you willing to cancel that "debt" today? Explain._____

_____

"It's their fault!" You may find yourself saying, "He makes me miserable," or "I can't do anything to make my life more enjoyable while I have to live with her." Blaming others leaves you in the powerless position of a victim. It also relieves you of responsibility for your emotional state, behavior, and success or failure. When you choose to stop blaming others for making you miserable, you accept responsibility for your life and become free to take steps to make yourself happier.

Whom do you blame for your troubles, and why? _____

_____

_____

Are you willing to take responsibility for your life, beginning today?

_____

_____

"I can make it on my own." You might have been neglected, hurt, and disappointed in ways that led you to develop an attitude of fierce independence. However, isolation is a choice usually born of a need for self-protection. An attitude that tells others to keep their distance can leave you lonely and depressed. Every human being needs to be loved and needs relationships with other people.

What steps can you take to overcome your self-isolation? _____

_____

_____

"If only . . ." Living in past pain or future fantasy can cause depression. Your past can become either a stumbling block or a stepping-stone, depending on how you choose to see it. Living in some fantasy future while doing nothing constructive can rob you of present blessing.

What is your "if only"? _____

_____

_____

If you released your regrets and set aside your fantasies to start living in the present, what problems would you need to face first?_____

_____

_____

"I deserve to be miserable." Taking on the martyr's attitude makes your state of depression into a relational weapon as well as a badge. You may find that you wear your moods to remind people of how much you have been through and to get them to be more lenient in their expectations of you. When you are depressed, the family may be more loving and patient. Some people become emotionally reliant on their state of depression to manipulate others into treating them better. This attitude may give you some small payback, but it leaves you depressed.

Will you make a decision to learn to give and receive love instead of trying to make people feel sorry for you in order to receive the loving response you need? (You may need the help of a counselor to help you act on this decision.)

_____

_____

_____

"I can never forgive them (or myself)." Unforgiveness, bitterness, and resentment can take over your life, leaving you emotionally exhausted and depressed. It has been said that bitterness is a cup of poison we drink. When you forgive, you are not saying what was done to you was acceptable. You are releasing yourself from having to carry the weight of emotion focused on what they did. You are handing the burden of avenging the wrong into the hands of God so that you can get on with your life. If you are holding unforgiveness against yourself, you must forgive yourself so that you don't stay miserable just because that is what you think you deserve.

DEPRESSION

First, complete this sentence: I forgive myself for _____
_____.

Now, fill in the blanks as follows:

I forgive _____ for _____.
I forgive _____ for _____.
I forgive _____ for _____.
I forgive _____ for _____.

(You may have to review this list when angry thoughts occasionally arise.)

"I'll never have enough." Being ungrateful for what you have is a downer. When you always see your glass as half empty instead of half full, you may choose to be depressed.

Will you choose to see life in a large enough perspective to appreciate what you have and express gratitude? List ten things for which you are grateful:

1. _____   6. _____
2. _____   7. _____
3. _____   8. _____
4. _____   9. _____
5. _____   10. _____

"I am powerless." You may not see any way to change particular situations. You may also believe you are powerless to change your attitudes and beliefs. You may believe that since life has been rotten to you, you are obligated to be miserable. You may have been overpowered so often in your life that being a victim and being characterized by the quality of powerlessness have become a part of your identity.

Are you willing to reach out to God in your powerlessness and allow his supernatural strength to flow into your human weakness? Write your thoughts.

_____

_____

Support Notes

Your loved one may not be seeing herself realistically and could possibly benefit from comparing your perspective to her own. If she feels comfortable enough to do this part of the action step, be courteous but honest. Think of specific instances that led you to your evaluation so that she doesn't lapse into feeling persecuted or attacked. Do not lecture her or try to persuade her to change. Simply offer your perspective if she asks. If she doesn't ask for your perspective but her evaluation seems out of touch with reality, tell her your observations, but don't try to make her change her evaluation.

Self-Talk

You may need to change the way you talk to yourself to fit with reality. For example, you may catch yourself saying something negative such as, "I knew today was going to be a miserable day," just because something bad happened. You can change this into a positive and realistic attitude by saying, "Yes, something bad happened, but I have a choice over whether I allow it to ruin my whole day."

Look at the negative attitudes and beliefs you identified as possible contributing factors to your depression. Which of them are related to things you have been taught?_____

_____

_____

_____

Who taught you these things?_____
_____

Are you willing to challenge your beliefs, try out some new theories about life, and learn to be optimistic? How do you plan to do this? _____
_____
_____

Are you willing to apply yourself to developing the skills you need to replace your negative attitudes and beliefs with more positive ones? _____
_____

Support Notes

You can be a positive influence today. Don't focus attention on the past negative attitudes and beliefs. Instead, show enthusiasm for the possibility of learning new ways of thinking. Since your loved one's negativity was probably developed through receiving negative input, your positive input is important. Encourage using books or tapes as a way to prime the pump for positive thinking.

Are You Dealing with Spiritual or Relational Issues?

Ask me, and I will tell you things that you don't know and can't find out.—Jeremiah 33:3 CEV

Spiritual Issues

Several spiritual issues can contribute to depression. Consider whether the following could be part of your problem:

- Alienation from God. You may feel distance between yourself and God. Perhaps you feel unworthy to be accepted by God, or you are at war with God for your own reasons. Either way, this alienation can be a burden to you.
- An area of sin from which you cannot break free. *Sin* means "to fall short of the mark." Violating your moral values can be quite distressing. That is especially true when you try to do what is right and find you continue to do the very things you don't believe in and don't want to do because they violate your moral standards.
- Demonic influence or oppression. Beliefs vary widely regarding the influence of unseen spiritual forces. Some people believe depression

can be caused or aggravated by being involved with the occult or experiencing ritualistic abuse.

- Living a double life. Making a public commitment to one set of values while secretly living another life can create a great deal of stress. Excessive stress can also occur if you present yourself dishonestly to the people near you and you have to keep up pretenses.

Rate yourself on a scale of 1 to 10 for how much you think each of these spiritual issues may contribute to your depression (1 means very little; 5 means a moderate influence; and 10 means a key contributing influence). List any other spiritual issues you see that may contribute to your depression, and rate them in the same way. Rate yourself on the following:

Spiritual Difficulty   Rating

Alienation from God   _____

An area of sin from which you cannot break free   _____

Demonic influence or oppression   _____

Living a double life   _____

Other spiritual issues: _____   _____

_____   _____

Support Notes

Spiritual issues touch to the core of a person's being. Your loved one may not feel comfortable discussing spiritual issues with you. If that is the case, respect his privacy in this matter. If he wants to talk about spiritual issues, try to be a source of comfort to him in whatever way you can without preaching, or refer him to a spiritual leader he respects.

Relational Issues

Sometimes relational problems and cycles leave you feeling stuck and depressed. Living in a situation where there is abuse, behavior that violates your conscience, neglect, or betrayal can bring about depression until you find a way to resolve your relational issues and move on with your life.

List the names of the people with whom you are having difficulties you believe could be contributing to your depression, and identify the problem in each relationship:

Person	Problem
1. _____	_____
2. _____	_____
3. _____	_____
4. _____	_____
5. _____	_____

Support Notes

If in discussing relational issues, your friend confides that he is being abused or that he is in danger from someone, take immediate action to get him appropriate help and protection. Don't leave him in the situation.

Dealing with Spiritual and Relational Issues

Spiritual and relational issues touch the heart and soul of your life. They can play a major role in developing depression. Even if these issues are not central to the cause of your depression, having a life-giving relationship with God and healthy relationships with loved ones can play a key role in your recovery. This is a great time to take steps to revitalize your relationships with God and loved ones.

Here are some suggestions for improving your spiritual life:

- Cry out to God. Ask him to receive you, guide you, and help you deal with all the issues contributing to your depression.
- Confess your sins. The Bible promises, "If we confess our sins, He [God] is faithful and just to forgive us our sins and to cleanse us from all unrighteousness" (1 John 1:9 NKJV). To confess simply means to agree with God about what he says is right and wrong. If you know that you have violated God's law and your own conscience, admit it. You don't have to be righteous before you do so. In fact, God says he will follow your confession with cleansing and give you his righteousness.
- Express the questions and emotions you dare not say out loud. You may have cut yourself off from God because he failed to live up to your expectations. You may have been hurt terribly or treated unjustly, and you struggle to understand how a loving God could allow such a thing to happen. You may feel tremendous anger toward God and simultaneously feel guilt or fear at the realization. God can handle your emotions and your doubts. Get them off your chest by expressing them in writing or with a spiritual counselor.
- Take your spiritual questions to someone who is professionally trained to have the answers. Just as you would hesitate to treat your own physical ailments or seek medical advice from someone who isn't trained in that field, don't take your spiritual questions to someone who isn't trained to understand life from a biblical perspective. Clarify your doubts and spiritual problems, then make an appointment with someone who has dedicated his or her life to serving God and teaching his ways.
- Seek forgiveness. Being forgiven is one of the most powerful remedies for the burdened soul. Seek forgiveness from God. Acknowledge

how you have hurt others, and seek to make amends, except when to do so would further hurt others.

- Treat yourself to something spiritually uplifting. If it has been a while since you have been able to enjoy a spiritual experience, plan to attend a positive spiritual event. A retreat on a positive theme, a Christian concert, or an uplifting worship service may remind you that there is joy in the house of God (and that you are welcome in his presence).

When difficult relationships contribute to your depression, you need to seek help that deals specifically with the problem you are having: marital difficulty, alcoholism or addiction within the family, communication problems, abusive treatment, parent-child issues, and so on. Once you have determined the central issues, you will be able to focus on finding help for you in your particular situation.

What kinds of relational problems relate to your depression?

_____

After discussing these problems with your support person, what steps do you think you should take to resolve these problems? _____

_____

_____

Support Notes

These are sensitive issues. Be especially careful to keep the confidences shared regarding spiritual and relational issues. If she isn't clear on the nature of relational problems, help her identify some related issues as a starting place. If she later feels the need to seek help for relational issues, she will be able to gain a fuller picture in the process regardless of where she starts.

Unraveling a Mystery Depression

[The Word of God] discovers the desires and thoughts of our hearts.
—Hebrews 4:12 CEV

If you have gone through the exercises in the last few pages and feel as though you're grasping at straws because the possible contributing factors do not seem to apply to your situation, you are dealing with a mystery that needs to be solved.

Sometimes depression can be an indicator of repressed trauma. Perhaps a factor contributing to your depression is something deeply hidden. It may be something so terrible that you are trying to forget it or push it out of your mind. It may be something so deeply devastating that your mind has hidden it away from you. There are cases where repressed trauma results in depression. These cases often involve some form of extreme violence and/or sexual abuse. It is important to note that this is a very controversial subject, and it is wise to address it with professional assistance.

Are you aware of anything traumatic or abusive that happened to you or someone you love that you are trying not to think about? Explain.

_____

_____

Are there large gaps in your memory about your life? _____

_____

Are you willing to consider the possibility of a repressed trauma contributing to your depression if you are unable to identify any other contributing factors?

_____

_____

_____

If you are hiding a terrible secret, or if you have no recollection of abuse but periods of time are missing from your memory, your mystery depression may be a cry for help from within. If you cannot find identifiable causes and solutions for your depression by completing this journey, it would be in your best interest to seek professional help. Perhaps you have had an experience that was so traumatic, your mind completely blocked it out from your consciousness. If that is the case, a good therapist with a proven track record working with repressed trauma and those who have been victims of abuse can help you determine if your mystery depression may be a clue to something deeper that needs to be resolved.

Do you have any reason to believe that your depression may be partially caused by some experience of abuse or trauma? Explain. _____

_____

_____

If this seems to be a possibility, ask your support person to help you find a therapist who can give you professional assistance in exploring the possibility.

Support Notes

If your friend is at a loss concerning the source of her depression, encourage her to get a diagnosis from a therapist who specializes in dealing with repressed trauma. There is nothing to lose. Strong resistance to the idea may indicate a problem she is afraid to face. If your friend begins to remember flashes of traumatic or shameful experiences, reaffirm your acceptance, love, and support. Do not try to handle the problem on your own! Get professional help. If she tells you about specific acts of abuse or identifies her abuser, listen compassionately. If she is living in a dangerous situation, take steps immediately to provide protection. Never minimize or cover up abuse. It bears repeating: *get help immediately*.

Creating Your Personal Treatment and Recovery Plan

Those who trust in the LORD will find new strength. . . . They will walk and run without getting tired.—Isaiah 40:31 CEV

Recovery from depression can constitute a major project. Just because it seems monumental does not mean that it is unreachable; you merely need to give yourself some time and rearrange your life to deal with the issues you have discovered to be contributing to your depression.

Are you willing to rearrange your life in a way that allows you to deal with the issues contributing to your depression? How do you feel about doing so?

_____

_____

_____

Are you willing to set aside a block of time each week to focus on resolving the issues that contribute to your depression? What is your reaction to doing so?

_____

_____

_____

Are you willing to make a long-term commitment to deal with the time-consuming issues you have discovered in this part, which will take time to resolve?

_____

_____

Are you willing to allow someone you trust to encourage you and hold you accountable to continue your recovery? Who? _____

_____

_____

If you do not already have one, draw up a written schedule of how you currently spend your time. (We'll do this in more detail later in the workbook.) Then rearrange your commitments in such a way that reserves the time you need to continue making investments in your recovery and self-nurturing.

Put the specific commitment of time you are willing to make into writing along with your signature. Allow your support person to witness your commitment, and ask the person to encourage you and hold you accountable to continue living in recovery from your depression.

If you have not already done so, turn to page 41 in Part 1 and read the material on finding and accessing resources and support. Follow the steps outlined to begin creating your personal treatment and recovery plan for depression.

Support Notes

Your long-term commitment to support your loved one will help him find the courage to make this life-changing commitment. Be sure to take your commitment to him as seriously as you take his commitment to recovery.

Setting Boundaries to Uphold Your Happiness

Wisdom brings strength, and knowledge gives power.
—Proverbs 24:5 CEV

Once your depression lifts, you can do several things to uphold your happiness. They involve setting boundaries to protect yourself from falling prey to the factors that contributed to your depression. Clearly define these boundaries now. When these boundaries are crossed, sound the alarm to bring your life back within the limits of what you know to be healthy for you. That will protect you from further pain. Consider diet, high-stress situations, isolation, overly negative input, and any other factors you have discovered, and identify your healthy boundaries.

The important thing is that you don't start to take your health and happiness for granted and stop doing the things that restored your health.

Make a list of ten limits you believe will keep you in general good health: for example, I will get eight hours of sleep each night, I will not work more than forty-five hours each week, and so on.

1._____

2._____

3. _____

4. _____

5. _____

6. _____

7. _____

8. _____

9. _____

10. _____

Make another list of the specific things related to the particular factors contributing to your depression that you need to guard as being vital to maintain your emotional health.

1. _____

2. _____

3. _____

4. _____

5. _____

6. _____

7. _____

8. _____

9. _____

10. _____

Share these lists with your support person, and ask for help in noticing when you are crossing the line.

Support Notes

As time passes and the depression lifts, it is easy to grow lax in doing the things that preserve physical and emotional health. If you notice signs of fatigue or symptoms of depression, bring them up for discussion. Your loved one may become defensive, so be careful not to approach the issue with a condemning attitude. However, if she asks you to help her remain free of depression, lovingly present what you see happening. Ultimately, it is her choice, but she might be helped by your willingness to sound the alarm if you notice the boundaries being overstepped.

Accepting Full Responsibility for Your Life Again

Are any of you wise or sensible? Then show it by living right and by being humble and wise in everything you do.—James 3:13 CEV

While you are suffering from depression, you will be affected to some degree in ways that limit your ability to fulfill your responsibilities. Just as with any other illness, you should grant yourself some leeway while you are suffering from the condition and recovering. However, a time will come when you will be healthy enough to accept full responsibility for your life.

Here are some questions you can ask yourself about when, what, and how to do this:

What responsibilities belong to you when you are in good health that you have been limited in fulfilling while depressed? _____

_____

_____ _____

Which people have taken on some measure of your responsibility while you are unable to carry it?_____

_____

Are you willing to acknowledge their contribution and enlist their help as you move toward gradually accepting full responsibility for your life again? Explain.

_____

_____

_____

Support Notes

You will be in a position to gauge if this is something your loved one is ready to deal with now. Not everyone will be by the end of this workbook, and that is okay. If your loved one is still working through deeply rooted issues, his season of being down and unable to assume full responsibility for life may be necessarily prolonged. If that is the case, your role is to encourage him that his health is not yet restored to the point where he needs to resume his responsibilities. If you sense he is ready, work with any counselors involved or directly with him to make the transition as smooth as possible. It will take time to get back into the habit of taking care of his life and resume his responsibilities to others.

Appreciating the Value of Sorrow and Pain

I will comfort them and turn their sorrow into happiness.
—Jeremiah 31:13 CEV

Even after you have recovered from depression, you cannot expect life to be painless. Life in this world involves loss, death, disappointment, failure, disease, sorrow, and pain. No one is exempt. What makes the difference is how you learn to deal with the sorrow and pain that come your way. Sorrow and pain are not always without redeeming value. If you learn to appreciate sorrow and pain, they can have some positive effects. Here are some examples of how sorrow and pain can help you:

- Sorrow and pain can draw you closer to loved ones. In your times of sorrow you can discover the love and compassion of those who truly care about you. You may also see false friends fall away. After your depression is over, you will have a few friends you know to be tried and true.

- Sorrow and pain can act as purifying agents in life. You may experience sorrow and pain as the results of wrong behavior. They can act as a purifying fire, causing you to eliminate harmful behavior that results in pain to yourself and others.

- Sorrow and pain can draw attention to areas in your body or your life that need care. Just as physical pain can lead a surgeon to the part of the body needing treatment, your emotional pain can draw attention to areas of your life where something needs to be corrected or healed.

- Sorrow and pain can remind you to look toward eternity. Although you will never completely escape them while you are living in an earthly body, they help you focus your desire on an eternal home where sorrow and pain will be relieved. The Bible promises that your eternal home is a place where God "will wipe away every tear from their eyes; there shall be no more death, nor sorrow, nor crying. There shall be no more pain" (Rev. 21:4 NKJV).

Look back over your experiences during your season of intense pain and while recovering from it. What of redeeming value can you glean from these experiences? Before you write, discuss the question with your support person.

_____

_____

_____

Support Notes

Anyone coming out of depression will need to accept that life will hold some pain. This reality may be especially frightening for those who have been overwhelmed by depression. At some point encourage discussion of what marks the difference between accepting the routine sorrow and pain life serves up and succumbing to depression. If you have not resolved these issues for yourself, it will be helpful for you to do so before discussing them with your loved one.

Well Done!

Congratulations. You have completed Part 3 of *The Emotional Freedom Workbook*. Before you move on to the final part, write down the three most important lessons you have learned about beating the blues.

1. _____

2. _____

3. _____

Part 4

Procrastination

No matter what I'm doing, I have this guilty feeling that I should be doing something else instead. I've got a million responsibilities, and I don't know what to do first. Sometimes I just sit and stare at the TV when I know I should be working. I'm afraid to start anything because I know I'll never finish it.—Howard T.

Procrastination keeps you from starting, working on, or finishing important tasks. It is sometimes joked about, often trivialized, and occasionally applauded, but procrastination damages relationships, aborts valuable projects, and sometimes devastates the future. In short, procrastination is a spoiler.

Putting things off may reflect other problems as well, such as fear, exhaustion, depression, or anger. By looking at the reasons you put things off, you make valuable discoveries about yourself, which will make you willing to try, to persevere, and to finish what you've started. Procrastination, harmless and insignificant as it may seem, nearly always slows you down on your way to emotional freedom.

Are You a Procrastinator?

Wisdom brings success.—Ecclesiastes 10:10 NKJV

Most people put things off from time to time. But if procrastinating becomes a habit, it can hold you captive, preventing you from living life to the fullest, from reaching your goals, and from having peace of mind. If procrastination is one of the things that block your way to emotional freedom, you will find this part helpful. You may also find that procrastination interacts with some of the other parts of this workbook. It can contribute to your feelings of shame. It can involve your behavior in unhealthy relationships. It can also contribute to depression. Even if there is something else you really "should" be doing, take the time to reflect and write responses to the following questions.

When do you tend to procrastinate? _____

_____

_____

In what ways would you feel better about yourself and your life if you didn't procrastinate? _____

_____

_____

_____

PROCRASTINATION

What matters would you be able to face right now without hesitation?

_____

_____

How would this benefit you?_____

_____

_____

What negative consequences of procrastinating would you avoid?

_____

_____

An old joke says, "I'm going to stop procrastinating—tomorrow." But why do you procrastinate? Most procrastinators ask themselves that question again and again. There are several reasons for putting off until tomorrow what you should do today:

- Procrastination is often associated with obligation: things you feel you have to do, should do, or are expected to do. When you feel pulled between what you should do and what you want to do, you are inclined to procrastinate.
- Procrastination may be associated with doubt about whether a decision or action is right or wrong. While you wrestle with the issue, time is slipping away.
- You may procrastinate because other things seem more important, and you have difficulty prioritizing.
- You may procrastinate because of fear of failure or success. You may fear that failure to reach a goal would cause you and others to see you as a failure. If you succeed, you may fear being expected to succeed continually.

No matter how much you procrastinate, there are some situations in which you never do. What are ten things you do each day without hesitation?

1._____
2._____
3._____
4._____
5._____
6._____
7._____
8._____
9._____
10._____

Reflect on each of these things you do not procrastinate in doing. Determine whether each situation fits one or more of the following descriptions, and mark it with 1, 2, 3, and/or 4 accordingly:

1. It is something you choose to do and/or want to do.

2. It is something you accept as being okay or right.

3. It is something that deserves your attention, even though you could spend your time on other things.

4. It is something that is not used to measure your worth or lack of worth, by yourself or others.

Now, identify examples from your life for each of the following:

I procrastinate when I _____

_____ because it feels like an obligation.

I procrastinate when I _____

_____ because I'm not sure it is okay to do it.

PROCRASTINATION

I procrastinate when I _____
_____ because other things seem more important to do first.

I procrastinate when I _____
_____ because it involves a goal, and I fear finding out how
I will measure up.

Think about the common denominators among the things you do not procrastinate over. What clues might that give you about why you procrastinate over certain things and not others?_____
_____
_____

Procrastination Serves Your Purposes

He that lies upon the ground cannot fall.—Yiddish proverb

You are probably accustomed to thinking of procrastination as a problem. For the moment, consider how procrastination has been a useful tool.

Once you realize that procrastination serves your purposes, it loses some of its mystery. Once you identify the purpose(s) being served by procrastination, you will be in a much better position to eliminate the habit and replace it with a suitable alternative. In some instances you may even decide that procrastination works to your advantage and elect to continue taking delayed action as a preferred response to specific circumstances.

Here are some ways procrastination can serve specific purposes. Place a check mark next to any of these that describe how procrastinating has served you:

___ Helps you sort out what is important to you.

___ Helps you avoid issues and situations that could prove painful, embarrassing, shameful, or difficult.

___ Allows you to avoid coming face-to-face with your human flaws.

___ Helps you remain in the comfort of the familiar, avoiding failure or the changes associated with possible failure.

___ Is a useful way of communicating feelings (such as resentment, anger, disappointment, or sadness) that you would never put into words.

___ Is a way of gaining power over someone in a position of power over you.

___ Allows you to get out of doing something you didn't want to do.

___ Provides you with a buffer between yourself and discovering the best of your ability.

___ Allows you to make promises with the chance of not having to follow through.

___ Keeps you from being overwhelmed.

___ Keeps you from making a wrong decision by making no decision.

___ Gives you enjoyment when you feel you are being deprived in your daily commitments.

___ Protects you from facing activities and situations that trigger unresolved emotional issues.

___ Allows you to put things off, then rush to achieve whatever is required, just in the nick of time.

___ Puts you under pressure so you can function in a high-stress mode, using fear and adrenaline as fuel.

___ Other: _____

For each item you checked, describe one example from your life: What did you procrastinate, and how did it serve that particular purpose?

1. _____

2. _____

3. _____

4. _____

5. _____

Learning to Choose

All changes, even the most longed for, have their melancholy; for what we leave behind us is a part of ourselves; we must die to one life before we can enter into another.—Anatole France

Daily life requires making choices, moment by moment, of what you will do now, postpone until later, or not do at all.

Here are some choices that can help you stop procrastinating:

Choose to expect less of yourself in a given time frame. If you consistently schedule too little time to accomplish your tasks, you will repeatedly have to put things off or get time extensions. In this way, you set yourself up to look like a procrastinator. By choosing to lower your expectations or by giving yourself more time to reach your self-imposed goals, you will reduce the need to put off other routine commitments.

Decide how you want to live your life. Procrastination seems to be a problem only when you put off things that conflict with your stated commitments and values. Maybe the real problem is that the values you espouse are not really your own. Therefore, when it comes to carrying through on the work involved, you lack the internal motivation.

You may be trying to live to please someone else or to fulfill another's dreams for you. For example, let's say your parents always wanted you to become a doctor, and they sacrificed their resources to put you through medical school. However, you discover that the field of medicine holds little interest for you. You may go along with their dreams for you on a superficial level, but you may experience an inner resistance to doing the work involved in completing medical training. You may chronically procrastinate when it comes to your studies.

Choose to trade, delegate, and dump some duties. If you dislike taking out the garbage, negotiate with others in your family to trade duties. Ask them what chore they dislike and see if you can make a trade with someone who is not as reluctant to take out the trash. You can also choose to delegate the tasks you really don't want to do.

Choose to hire someone to do the things you keep putting off. Services are available to do almost anything you can think of, including cleaning out your garage, handling your taxes, reorganizing your closet, and shopping for groceries. If costs are prohibitive, consider using the services of neighborhood teens or bartering services.

Choose to redefine commitments more realistically. If you have promised to do things that you are now putting off because you have overcommitted your time, energy, or money, you can choose to redefine the commitments. This may mean sincerely apologizing for making a promise you cannot keep at this season of your life or rescheduling your commitment for a realistic time in the future.

Choose to lower the stakes. If you tell yourself a task must be perfect, if your self-esteem is at stake, you will hesitate to begin, or you will have a hard time knowing when enough is enough. You may focus so much time and attention on one task that others have to be postponed.

For each of the choices listed, identify one area where you procrastinate that might be helped by making the choice described here. (You don't have to commit to change; just identify the possibility.) _____

_____

_____

Which of the choices do you feel most comfortable with? _____

_____

Explain. _____

_____

_____

Give Yourself Some Slack

There is a difference between
striving for excellence,
and striving for perfection.
The first is attainable, gratifying
and healthy.
The second is unattainable,
frustrating and neurotic.
It is also a terrible waste of time.—*Edwin Bliss*

People who tend to procrastinate are often perfectionists. If you measure your self-esteem by how well you produce or perform, it is no wonder that the important things in life, the things you value most, seem to be the most difficult to face. You can help yourself kick the procrastination habit by giving yourself some slack. Here are some specific ways:

- Consider whether perfectionism is an issue you need to redefine. No one is perfect. If you hold to standards of perfection that are unrealistically demanding, take time to challenge the assumptions you have accepted. Seriously contemplate why you feel you must be perfect. When you get to the bottom of the issues, you will be able to give yourself some slack.

- Understand and accept your personality and personal style. Try not to compare yourself with others and expect to perform as they do. You have a unique personality. While some personality types find it easy to meticulously attend to details and follow one project through to completion before making another commitment, other personality types tend to become interested in many things and are easily distracted.

- Understand and accept your internal time clock. If you are a night person who has bursts of creativity in the evening hours, don't condemn yourself when you can't get going in the morning. Instead, accept your unique rhythms, and try to set up your work schedule to make the most of the times when you are at your best.

Do you judge your value on the basis of who you are or on how you perform?

_____

Would you call yourself a perfectionist? _____

_____

If yes, are you proud of your perfectionism? Explain._____

_____

_____

_____

Do you see that perfectionism could be a symptom of a problem? Explain.

_____

_____

How does your unique personality type relate to your tendency to procrastinate?

_____

_____

PROCRASTINATION

How does your body clock affect your procrastination?_____

_____

_____

What would happen if you placed fewer demands on yourself when you are not

at peak performance? _____

_____

_____

Neglect, Avoidance, or Refusal?

If you want to live, give up your foolishness and let understanding guide your steps.—Proverbs 9:6 CEV

There are varying degrees of procrastination and various underlying issues that create the need to procrastinate. If you can discover what is behind your tendency to procrastinate in a particular area, you will have a much better chance of coming up with an appropriate response. We have divided procrastination patterns into three general categories: (1) things you neglect to do, (2) things you avoid, and (3) things you refuse to take responsibility for.

Neglect refers to things that you never seem to have time to do and you don't really feel troubled about them.

Avoidance refers to things that you don't do because of feelings of fear, pain, sadness, or other unpleasant emotions.

Refusal refers to things that you have determined not to do—you will not deal with certain aspects of life or accept responsibility for particular tasks.

As quickly as possible, list as many things as you can that fall into each category. Don't take a lot of time—just note each idea in the category that seems to fit the closest.

PROCRASTINATION

Neglect	Avoidance	Refusal
_____	_____	_____
_____	_____	_____
_____	_____	_____
_____	_____	_____
_____	_____	_____
_____	_____	_____

Now consider your responses:

- The things you neglect may reveal what you actually believe to be unworthy of your time and effort.
- The things you avoid may give clues about areas of life where you have been wounded.
- The things you refuse to do can point out some of the relationships where you are actively involved in a power struggle. When you dare to go beyond dealing with the symptoms to dealing with underlying causes, you are moving in the direction of emotional freedom. Dare to look deeper!

Streamlining Your Life

There cannot be a crisis next week. My schedule is already full.
—Henry Kissinger

In our fast-paced, complex, technologically sophisticated society there is an overload of information and options. You have responsibilities related to each role you play: employer/employee, parent, child, family member, church member, citizen, and so on. You are confronted with political issues on local, state, national, and international levels. You are faced with needs from all over the globe, from children starving in developing countries to environmental issues that are reported to threaten the continued existence of the planet. For each of these problems, someone is telling you that you should care and do something to combat them. You are bombarded with requests for charitable donations on a local level as well, many of which seem worthy of your support.

The Solution? Streamlining

Identify what is of minor importance in this season of your life. If you are raising small children, you may decide that for this season you are not going to focus on maintaining a demanding social calendar. If you are busy building your career, you may decide that personally maintaining your lawn just doesn't rate high enough for you to do it yourself.

PROCRASTINATION

Take obligations off your mental list. When you determine that something is of minor importance to you at this time, you are not saying that it has no value. If you still have a sense of obligation to something on your list of minor importance, consider giving of your resources instead of your time.

Find more efficient ways to accomplish necessary things. If cooking nutritious, homemade meals for your family is important to you, you may be able to find ways to accomplish this goal in a shorter amount of time. By changing your everyday routine, you can save more time to use in other ways.

Get rid of possessions that require too much upkeep. Perhaps you don't need the big executive house now that the kids have moved out—a condominium would involve less work. Or maybe the boat isn't as much fun as it used to be, and it's costing you time and money you would rather spend elsewhere.

After reflecting on the points just noted, try to answer these questions as thoughtfully as possible:

What are some things that seem of minor importance to you during this season of life, which you nevertheless have felt obligated to continue?

1. _____
2. _____
3. _____
4. _____

What are some obligations you could remove from your calendar?

1. _____
2. _____
3. _____
4. _____

What are some things you do as a part of your routine that you could do more efficiently?

1. _____
2. _____

3. _____

4. _____

Which possessions may not be worth the amount of time they require?

1. _____

2. _____

3. _____

4. _____

Confused or Conflicting Priorities

To everything there is a season,
A time for every purpose under heaven.
—Ecclesiastes 3:1 NKJV

If your priorities are confused, you will continually struggle with procrastination. When you are not certain what is important to you, you will lack guidelines that could allow you to put things off with a clear conscience. Without clearly defining priorities, you always have the sense that you are probably not spending your time in the right way, but you are never sure.

When are you confused over whether there is something more important to do than what you are doing? Think back over the past week and cite a specific example. _____

_____

_____

What do you value in life? Rate each of these in order from 1 to 10 (1 means I don't value or it doesn't apply to me; 10 means most valuable):

Family relationships _____

Marriage _____

Friendships   _____

Dating   _____

Parenting   _____

Career/work   _____

Hobbies   _____

Political involvement   _____

Civic involvement   _____

Education   _____

Recreation   _____

Faith and spirituality   _____

Physical fitness   _____

Creating and managing your home   _____

Paying bills/dealing with finances   _____

Study the list of items. Place a check mark next to each item if you can recall a time when you experienced confusion over whether you should be doing that task or another important task.

Place a star next to each item if you tend to procrastinate before you get started. Take special note if you are thinking that you should be doing something else but you are confused about which to do first.

Circle any items that seem to be in conflict, and draw a line connecting the two circles.

When do you experience a conflict between priorities that you value?

_____

_____

How does this relate to your tendency to procrastinate? _____

_____

_____

PROCRASTINATION

Do you use your time to do things you really value? _____

_____

If not, is it because of economic necessity? _____

_____

Are you adapting your life to please someone else? Explain. _____

_____

_____

What can you do to plan for a future where you will be better able to spend your time on things you value? _____

_____

_____

Time Out: Overcommitted and Undernourished

Remember the Sabbath day, to keep it holy. Six days you shall labor and do all your work, but the seventh day is the Sabbath of the LORD your God. . . . For in six days the LORD made the heavens and the earth, the sea, and all that is in them, and rested the seventh day. Therefore the LORD blessed the Sabbath day and hallowed it.—Exodus 20:8–11 NKJV

Every human being needs time to nourish body, mind, and spirit. For some reason, taking this time doesn't seem to come naturally. If it did, God probably wouldn't have had to command the human race to take one day each week to rest from work, to refresh themselves, and to renew their relationship with God. Just as nature shows you there are times to grow, to decline, to wake, and to sleep, you need to find a balance in life that allows for physical, emotional, mental, and spiritual ebb and flow.

Describe a time when you procrastinated in order to give yourself a much-needed break. _____

_____

_____

_____

PROCRASTINATION

What time do you set aside each week to do things that nourish you physically, emotionally, mentally, and spiritually?_____
_____

If you were able to set aside all of today's demands, what would you say you need to do for your own well-being? _____
_____

List ten specific things you need to do to function at peak performance level (examples might include get eight hours of sleep, take vitamins, exercise, etc.):

1._____
2._____
3._____
4._____
5._____
6._____
7._____
8._____
9._____
10._____

If you were to do these things every day, would you feel more able to accomplish some of the things you've been putting off? Give an example.
_____
_____

Imagine and describe how your life could be better one year from now if you would guard some time each day and one day each week to nourish yourself.
_____
_____

The Problem
of Pain

No pain, no gain.—Motto at gym

No one wants to hurt. People avoid physical pain by postponing visits to the dentist or necessary surgery. People who have experienced severe sexual, physical, or emotional trauma are known to postpone the emotional pain of dealing with what happened to them by completely blocking the awareness of the experience from their consciousness. Putting things off may be your way to avoid getting too close to your emotional pain. Not everything you procrastinate about hides a wound. However, if the reason for procrastination is a mystery, there is a good chance that it may be a means of avoiding the threat of pain.

You may want to overcome procrastination, but you may not be interested in groping around for underlying causes. In fact, if there are some hidden emotional injuries in your life, you will probably recoil at the thought of poking around where it might hurt. However, once the deeper issue is dealt with, there will be no reason for you to continue procrastinating in this area.

What are you procrastinating about right now? _____

_____

_____

_____

PROCRASTINATION

What do you procrastinate over because you are hesitant to deal with the pain involved?_____

_____

_____

Are you putting off something right now because you fear it will hurt?

_____

Are there some things you procrastinate over that are a mystery to you? Do you experience a vague uneasiness or irrational resistance when you think about doing them? _____

_____

_____

Take some time to think about how you feel about facing your fears. Then write your thoughts. Notice which areas cause you the most concern. If you gain insight into what you may be afraid of and why, note these things for your information._____

_____

_____

_____

Avoiding Embarrassment and Shame

Then the eyes of both of them were opened, and they knew that they were naked; and they sewed fig leaves together and made themselves coverings. . . . Then the LORD God called to Adam and said to him, "Where are you?" So he said, "I heard Your voice in the garden, and I was afraid because I was naked; and I hid myself."—Genesis 3:7, 9 NKJV

Embarrassment and shame are similar, yet different. For our purposes, let's define embarrassment as an uncomfortable feeling associated with something you do that is socially unacceptable. Shame (as we learned in Part 1) is also an uncomfortable emotion, but the distinction is that shame is associated with some socially unacceptable flaw in who you are, not just what you do.

- Embarrassment occurs when you make a mistake.
- Shame occurs when you believe *you* are a mistake.

Both the desire to avoid embarrassment and the need to cover unhealthy internal shame have power to trigger procrastination.

PROCRASTINATION

1. What experiences can you recall where you were embarrassed?

_____

2. Can you think of subsequent situations where you procrastinated in an attempt to avoid being embarrassed in that way again?_____

_____

3. What is there about you that you fear may be flawed? _____

_____

4. Where did your feelings of being flawed or inadequate originate?

_____

_____

5. Who pointed out that there was something wrong with you?

_____

6. Have you ever challenged those shameful assumptions? _____

_____

7. What do you procrastinate over that may be associated with the shameful belief that someone may discover your secret flaws?_____

_____

Explain. _____

_____

_____

If questions 3 through 7 revealed to you that you are struggling with shame, we strongly recommend that you complete Part 1 of this workbook.

Fear of Failure, Fear of Success

What we must decide is perhaps how we are valuable rather than how valuable we are.—Edgar Z. Friedenberg

Fear of failure and fear of success are two of the most common causes of procrastination. Anytime you undertake a task, you risk both failure and success. You may find life more comfortable if you procrastinate whenever faced with such a risk. Here are some perceived risks you may associate with the possibility of failure:

- Damaged self-esteem. Some people are secure in their inherent worth as human beings and accept occasional failure as a normal part of the human condition. Other people do not accept themselves as valuable unless they are continually doing something to prove their worth.

- Loss of employment. If your boss says she is watching you to judge whether you are doing your job effectively, it is understandable that you may hesitate at any project that could be used to determine your standing in the company.

- Loss of status. If you are trying to please someone with your performance, you may balk at efforts that would measure how well you compare to the person's ideal of you. For example, if your dad always dreamed that you would be the all-star quarterback in college, you may procrastinate in trying out for the team because this test will determine whether you are able to please your father.

There are also some perceived risks you may associate with the fear of success:

- Resentment of success. If you succeed, there is the risk that others may resent your success and stop associating with you in a positive way. Single women may fear that great financial success may intimidate potential suitors. Married women may fear that if their success exceeds that of their husbands, it will lead to marital difficulties. Men who become highly successful may fear that they will no longer fit in with the group of guys they grew up with. Some family members resent and ridicule success that sets one sibling in a higher social standing than others.
- Unclear relationships. If you succeed, you may not be sure whether people who claim to love you and care about you are sincere or merely want to be associated with someone successful.
- Overwhelming expectations. If you succeed and ascend to a higher position in your work, you may fear that more will be expected of you until you become overwhelmed.
- Changed lifestyle. If you succeed, your way of life would change, and you may fear leaving your current situation where you feel confident and comfortable.

When do you experience fear of failure? _____

_____

Why? _____

_____

If you fail at something, what conclusions does that cause you to draw about yourself? _____

_____

_____

_____

How is fear of failure associated with your procrastination habit?

_____

_____

_____

In what endeavors do you experience a fear of success?_____

_____

_____

_____

Why? _____

_____

_____

_____

In what specific ways do you procrastinate to keep yourself from experiencing the success you could achieve if you gave your best performance?

_____

_____

_____

In the left column, list anything you procrastinate over because of a fear of failure; in the right column, list all the negative consequences that you suppose would happen if you were to fail at that particular task:

PROCRASTINATION

Fear of failure keeps me from

If I fail, I'm afraid of

_____   _____

_____   _____

_____   _____

_____   _____

_____   _____

Now, in the left column, list anything you procrastinate over because of a fear of success; in the right column, list all the negative consequences that you suppose would happen if you were to succeed at that particular task:

Fear of success keeps me from

If I succeed, I'm afraid of

_____   _____

_____   _____

_____   _____

_____   _____

_____   _____

Choose one item from your fear of failure list and one item from your fear of success list. Close your eyes and try to imagine some way you could live comfortably with yourself if you were to fail or succeed in each area. For example, imagine failing a test and having your teacher offer to help you learn the concepts you don't understand. Or imagine being given a promotion and your friends congratulating you. Write your thoughts about what you imagined.

_____

_____

Monsters in the Dark: Fear of the Unknown

We should not let our fears hold us back from pursuing our hopes.
—John F. Kennedy

Remember how childhood fears of monsters in the dark could paralyze you and keep you from getting a needed drink of water? Fear of the unknown may still paralyze some people, keeping them from moving ahead on even simple tasks.

A story is told of a farmer who mowed around a large flat stone in his field. Each year he fretted over the added work involved in having to carefully maneuver around the stone that kept him from using his entire field for crops. He assumed, from the breadth of the stone, that it went down deep into the earth, so he procrastinated about moving it. After years of putting off the task, he finally got out the backhoe and tried to move the stone. It moved easily. He could have moved the one-inch-thick stone by hand. Yet he had limited his productivity because he hesitated to confront the unknown "monster."

Sometimes you may put off attempting something like a minor repair or a visit to the doctor or a financial investment because you assume that it will be a major undertaking. You may become overwhelmed with your assumption while the true level of difficulty remains a mystery.

PROCRASTINATION

Identify five things that you put off because of the unknown:

1. _____
2. _____
3. _____
4. _____
5. _____

For each item, list everything you need to know before you could complete it:

1. _____
   _____
2. _____
   _____
3. _____
   _____
4. _____
   _____
5. _____
   _____

In many cases you will discover, as the farmer did in moving the stone, that gaining information about the situation will lead to a simple way to accomplish tasks that at first seem overwhelming or intimidating. Dare to try to lift the stones in your way.

The Silent Power of Procrastination

God's Spirit doesn't make cowards out of us. The Spirit gives us power, love, and self-control.—2 Timothy 1:7 CEV

When procrastination is used in a power struggle, it can be an effective tool, perhaps even a weapon. In situations where you lack overt power, you may find considerable power in procrastinating.

Here are some examples:

- A child or adolescent may take his time in complying with a parent's command in an attempt to convey his independence and perhaps his anger.
- An employee may feign submission to a tyrannical boss while continuing a pattern of being late for work and taking her time in doing her job.
- When a spouse is being required to do something, he or she may put it off while smiling and saying, "Yes, Dear, I'll get to that soon." What is really meant is, "I will get around to it when I choose or when you show me enough respect to ask instead of demand."

In what ways does procrastination give you a sense of power in situations where someone has power over you? _____
_____

PROCRASTINATION

When have you used the silent power of procrastination to convey a message or emotional statement that you were unwilling to state verbally?

_____

_____

What results did you achieve? _____

_____

_____

Does using procrastination as a means of exerting your power have negative consequences for you? _____

_____

It isn't always a bad idea to use procrastination to help you in a power struggle if it will serve your purpose and is your best alternative. Sometimes it provides an unspoken "time out" and an opportunity for thought and preparation. However, make sure that your choice of procrastination instead of more direct means of communication doesn't hurt you and others.

Promising to Please: Thinking No But Saying Yes

Who cannot resolve upon a moment's notice to live his own life, he forever lives a slave to others.—Gotthold Ephraim Lessing

If you have the tendency to say yes at times when you really wish you could say no, you are setting yourself up to procrastinate. If you gain a reputation as someone people can turn to whenever they need help, you will be frequently asked for assistance. A time will come when you will be overcommitted. Then you will procrastinate in the areas of your promises or in other areas so that you have time to fulfill your many commitments. You may also experience an undercurrent of resentment toward people who have asked for your help. If so, you will lack the internal motivation to follow through promptly with your commitment.

For many reasons people develop the habit of saying yes when they want to say no. Consider which of these may apply to you:

- You fear the consequences. In the movie *The Godfather*, the mobsters explained their "ability" to gain the cooperation of others by saying, "I made him an offer he couldn't refuse." That, of course, meant that the other person's life was on the line. There are times someone asks you to do something and you realize that saying no may have grave consequences—although probably not as grave as the godfather's.

- You feel it is part of your role to say yes. Phrases such as, "How can I refuse my own mother?" reflect unhealthy relationships that lock family members into saying yes when they want to say no.

- You want to be seen in a positive light. Some people cannot resist volunteering for every unwanted position or task up for grabs. If you try to please in every group, you quickly become overcommitted and have to procrastinate in order to juggle your commitments.

- You fear rejection. You may say yes out of your fear that the only way you can stay in everyone's good graces is to do what others want at all times. If this describes you, the time will come when you grow to resent the imbalances in your relationships. However, those to whom you say yes may not realize your true feelings since you probably hide them out of fear of rejection.

- You base your self-esteem and worth on the basis of what you do. Whenever you refuse someone, you feel that your value has diminished. When you please people by saying yes, you feel better about yourself.

- You feel indebted to the other person. If you have received substantial help from someone and you want to show your appreciation out of sincere gratitude, you will be able to say yes sincerely. If you feel indebted and therefore obligated to say yes, you may be feeling overpowered.

List five times when you said yes but wanted to say no:

1. _____

2. _____

3. _____

4. _____
5. _____

For each item you listed, why did you feel you had to say yes?
1. _____
2. _____
3. _____
4. _____
5. _____

What did you fear would happen if you said no?
1. _____
2. _____
3. _____
4. _____
5. _____

Overwhelmed by Reality

You may give out, but never give up.—Mary Crowley

In *Gone with the Wind*, Scarlett O'Hara repeatedly said, "I'll think about that tomorrow." For her, life was overwhelming, and the only way she knew to survive was to deal with as much as she could today and deal with the rest tomorrow.

Chances are slight that your world is crumbling in the way life in the Southern states crumbled during the Civil War. However, you may be overwhelmed by your reality: facing a failing marriage, handling a weighty workload, surviving financially, getting behind in school, grieving the death of a loved one, struggling with addictions. At times like these it is tempting to try to put off dealing with reality until you feel better able.

Here are some ways you may procrastinate when you feel overwhelmed by reality:

- You may abuse mood-altering substances such as drugs and alcohol. Drugs or alcohol may give you a temporary respite from life. But when chemical effects wear off, your problems are still there. They may even be compounded by things you did while under the influence.

- You may use mood-altering experiences. Having sex, working, eating, shopping, going to church, and pursuing other activities can distract you from your problems. These activities are not bad, but if they are used as an escape, they can become addictive or compulsive.

- You may pretend that everything is fine. Denial is a form of procrastination that buys you time by letting you believe nothing needs to be done. Families living with an alcoholic may pretend there isn't a problem. You may continue writing checks until you get a notice from the bank stating that your account is overdrawn. This act of denying financial reality allows you to put off cutting back on expenses, getting a better paying job, or selling one of your cars.

What are you currently doing to cope with a difficult life situation?

_____

_____

Are you doing anything that helps you put off dealing with reality?

_____

_____

What decisions are you afraid you might be required to make in order to deal with the reality of your situation? _____

_____

_____

Whom do you have to support you if you are in the midst of an overwhelming life situation?_____

_____

What (if any) mood-altering substances or experiences do you use to help you put off having to deal with your overwhelming reality?_____

_____

PROCRASTINATION

What are the negative side effects from your attempts to avoid facing your true situation? _____

_____

What are the momentary benefits?_____

_____

Acknowledging things that threaten to overwhelm you is quite a task. Allow yourself to respect the magnitude of whatever seems so overwhelming for you, talk to your chosen confidant(e), and don't belittle your valid fears. If something is powerful enough to cause you to put off facing the truth, it is worthy of your respect.

If some part of your life or past is overwhelming, try to write out what you find too much to bear. _____

_____

_____

_____

_____

Talk to your support person about your concerns. Together, make a list of your fears that keep you from facing life as it really is. Even when life seems overwhelming, there is always a way through. You can find your way if you are willing to summon your courage and get help to deal with whatever life has served you.

Dealing with Procrastination One Day at a Time

Take short steps. A lot of people fail because they try to take too big a step too quickly.—Zig Ziglar

What projects are you currently putting off because you don't have enough time in one sitting to complete the job? _____
_____

How could you break the job down into smaller, more manageable portions that would not be so intimidating? _____
_____

Do you tend to see procrastination as a problem or character flaw that is too big to overcome? Explain. _____
_____
_____
_____

    Many people who procrastinate focus on finishing the whole project instead of completing one step at a time. You may procrastinate in many different ways and for different reasons, some of which are deeply rooted. If you determine to rid yourself entirely of procrastination, you will set yourself up to be intimidated by the enormity of the assignment.

To effectively stop procrastinating, you need to tackle the problem in small, manageable doses. If you have completed the previous assignments, you are already dealing with procrastination by identifying some of the things that prompt your behavior. The remainder of your journey will take each view of procrastination you have already thought about and give you strategies for dealing with that aspect of your behavior.

"One day at a time" is a familiar slogan for people who use a twelve-step program to deal with addiction or other compulsive behaviors. It will be an important principle for you too.

Identify one specific task you would like to complete that will take a fairly long period of time. _____

_____

Think of one small part of this job that you could do in less than fifteen minutes. Set a timer and work for fifteen minutes. When the limited part of the project you selected is complete or when the timer goes off, stop. Continue this process, bit by bit, until the task is complete.

Do you think that with practice you could learn to approach other projects bit by bit rather than in large chunks?_____

_____

_____

If so, how will this affect your tendency to procrastinate? _____

_____

_____

The Realm of What's Okay

In a perfect world, you might be able to make perfect decisions. But we don't yet live in a perfect world.—Stephen Arterburn

Some people think there is one "right choice" for every decision. From that perspective, all other choices are wrong to varying degrees. These people look for the perfect will of God for their lives, Mr. or Ms. "Right," the perfect job, the perfect dress to wear to the reunion, and so on. The problem with this viewpoint is that it makes you hesitate before making any decision unless you are sure it is the right choice.

A more realistic view of life is to look for the realm of what is okay. In other words, be open to several acceptable possibilities. For example, in choosing a college you could look at location, areas of study, class size, and tuition to narrow the field to several acceptable choices in your realm of what is okay. In areas of moral conduct, you might use the Ten Commandments as your boundaries, which would tell you whether a particular decision was in the realm of what was okay. When you learn to view life as holding a multitude of choices, all of which are okay within specified boundaries, you are much more free to make decisions.

Do you often hesitate to make important decisions for fear that you may not make the "right choice"? Explain. _____

_____

_____

PROCRASTINATION

Identify one decision you are trying to make where you are concerned about making the "right choice." _____

_____

List your preferences, moral boundaries, and values regarding that choice:

Preferences	Moral Boundaries	Values
_____	_____	_____
_____	_____	_____
_____	_____	_____
_____	_____	_____
_____	_____	_____
_____	_____	_____
_____	_____	_____
_____	_____	_____
_____	_____	_____

Now that you have a wide range of options, list at least five that would be okay decisions:

1. _____

2. _____

3. _____

4. _____

5. _____

How do your feelings change about making a decision when you allow yourself to choose anything within the realm of what is okay rather than demand a perfect decision? _____

_____

Making Friends with Failure

The Creed of the Champion
I am not judged by the number of times I fail but by the number of times
I succeed, and the number of times I succeed is in direct proportion to the
number of times I can fail and keep on trying.—*Tom Hopkins*

Many people who procrastinate out of a fear of failure have been taught that failure in one specific area in life means failure at life. You may have learned at an early age that failure of any kind was totally unacceptable. You quickly learned to cover up your failures and pretend they never occurred. If that is what you have been taught to believe about failure, you need to reeducate yourself.

The fear of failure can actually hold you back from success. Many people who are renowned for being the best in their respective fields were, at times, the biggest failures in their fields. They were able to excel because they were willing to try and fail so many times.

A young reporter heard that Thomas Edison had failed more than ten thousand times in his attempts to invent the lightbulb. The reporter posed the question, "Mr. Edison, how does it feel to have failed so many times in one pursuit?" Thomas Edison replied, "My young man, I have not failed ten thousand times. I have successfully found ten thousand ways that will not work." The fact that you are probably reading this book by the light of an incandescent bulb illustrates the point that making friends with failure can lead to great success.

PROCRASTINATION

- Failure can be your teacher. As with Thomas Edison, failure is a means of gaining valuable knowledge of what will not work. By knowing clearly what doesn't work for you, you will more easily find the things that do work for you.
- Failure can encourage you to practice and refine. When you recognize that anyone who has learned to excel in any arena has practiced diligently, you will be more accepting of your perceived failures.
- Failure can give you an opportunity to develop your sense of humor. If you are able to laugh at yourself, you will enjoy life more. You will also find that you are more fun to be around.

Were you raised to believe that failure is a friend or a foe? _____

_____

_____

How do you feel about yourself when you fail? _____

_____

_____

Identify an area where you are afraid to try because you are afraid to fail.

_____

_____

Can you think of a time when failure has redirected your course?

_____

_____

Babe Ruth held the record for strikes as well as for home runs. What kind of attitude allowed him to swing with all his might? _____

_____

How would having a similar attitude toward the possibility of failure in your life allow you to overcome procrastination? _____

_____

_____

_____

Finding Your Success Comfort Zone

The important thing is this: to be able at any moment to sacrifice what we are for what we could become.—Charles Du Bos

How do you define success? _____

_____

_____

Ask your support person to define success, and write his or her definition here.

_____

_____

_____

In the areas of life where you have not yet reached what you define as success, what do you believe is standing in your way? _____

_____

_____

If you desire a brighter future that is markedly different from your past, but you procrastinate out of fear of change, you must find your success comfort zone. You do this by becoming familiar with success so that it becomes less threatening. Here are some ways to create a positive attitude toward success and create a success comfort zone:

- Educate yourself. What is life really like for people who have succeeded in ways you are afraid to succeed?
- Associate with successful people. If possible, join groups or make friends with people who are successful. Part of your fear of success may be that your friends might reject you if you succeed far beyond their accomplishments. If you develop friendships with people who are more successful than you are, you create your own positive peer pressure.
- Find mentors you want to emulate. Try to find someone who has a similar background to yours but who is now enjoying success.
- Read books. Learn about real people who have succeeded.
- Overcome your own objections. You have already identified what you fear may happen if you were to succeed. Review the objections and think of positive consequences of success.

Do you have any objections to becoming successful that you find impossible to overcome? Explain. _____

_____

If so, are you willing to talk the matter over with someone else who may be able to help you overcome your fear of success? Explain. _____

_____

Give yourself thirty minutes to daydream or imagine in glorious detail how your life and the lives of your loved ones could be improved if you were to stop procrastinating and allow yourself to be as successful as you can possibly be. Afterward, journal your thoughts and feelings. _____

_____

_____

Scheduling and Your Personal Boundaries

When you do the things you ought to do, when you ought to do them, the time will come when you can do the things you want to do, when you want to do them.—Zig Ziglar

Establishing personal boundaries in how you use your time can help you kick the procrastination habit. We recently saw this humorous notice posted in a place of business. This serves as an example of how inadequate boundaries in the use of time can result in feeling that you are procrastinating:

> **BUSINESS HOURS**
> OPEN Most Days About 9 or 10 Occasionally as Early as 7, But SOME DAYS as Late as 12 or 1. WE CLOSE About 5:30 or 6 Occasionally About 4 or 5, But Sometimes as Late as 11 or 12. SOME DAYS OR Afternoons, We Aren't Here at All, and Lately I've Been Here Just About All the Time, Except When I'm Someplace Else, But I Should Be Here Then Too.

Setting boundaries for the use of your time will help you find relief from the pressure of procrastination in several ways. For instance, you can draw the line between time to work and time to play. When it is time to play, you will know that you are not procrastinating about your work. You can also set aside a manageable portion of time for tasks that seem overwhelming. Instead of putting off a large task until you have a major block of time to complete it, mark out thirty minutes to spend on the task on specific days until the task is completed.

When you schedule specific blocks of time, you reduce interruptions. If someone suggests dropping by around three and you have a set schedule to work until five, you can say that you are not available until five. When you schedule activities, you are able to help others know when you are available to give them your full attention. Plus, you help yourself by cutting down on unexpected distractions.

Another benefit of scheduling is that you will not be shuffling details around. You may already schedule time for the important parts of your life such as work, school, church, and family time. But you may not schedule time for the routine duties such as paying bills, balancing your checking account, shopping, and running errands. If you give yourself time each week for the minor tasks, you won't be as likely to put them off.

Put your intended schedule in writing, and allow for each of the following:

Work
Play and relaxation each day
Weekly day of rest
Minor tasks

	MON	TUES	WED	THURS	FRI	SAT	SUN
6 A.M.	_____	_____	_____	_____	_____	_____	_____
7 A.M.	_____	_____	_____	_____	_____	_____	_____
8 A.M.	_____	_____	_____	_____	_____	_____	_____
9 A.M.	_____	_____	_____	_____	_____	_____	_____
10 A.M.	_____	_____	_____	_____	_____	_____	_____
11 A.M.	_____	_____	_____	_____	_____	_____	_____
12 noon	_____	_____	_____	_____	_____	_____	_____

PROCRASTINATION

	MON	TUES	WED	THURS	FRI	SAT	SUN
1 P.M.	_____	_____	_____	_____	_____	_____	_____
2 P.M.	_____	_____	_____	_____	_____	_____	_____
3 P.M.	_____	_____	_____	_____	_____	_____	_____
4 P.M.	_____	_____	_____	_____	_____	_____	_____
5 P.M.	_____	_____	_____	_____	_____	_____	_____
6 P.M.	_____	_____	_____	_____	_____	_____	_____
7 P.M.	_____	_____	_____	_____	_____	_____	_____
8 P.M.	_____	_____	_____	_____	_____	_____	_____
9 P.M.	_____	_____	_____	_____	_____	_____	_____
10 P.M.	_____	_____	_____	_____	_____	_____	_____
11 P.M.	_____	_____	_____	_____	_____	_____	_____
12 P.M.	_____	_____	_____	_____	_____	_____	_____

After your schedule is clearly defined, choose one project you have put off because it will be time consuming. Schedule fifteen minutes three times per week to work on the project. Set a timer and work only for the set time.

Think about how clarifying your personal time boundaries and communicating them to others can keep you from feeling that you are always procrastinating.

Making Amends

We cannot do everything at once, but we can do something at once.
—*Calvin Coolidge*

Your life is intertwined with the lives of others. Anytime you procrastinate, other people will be affected in some way. You may cause them a minor inconvenience, or you may have brought about a great amount of trouble because of your failure to do things in a timely manner. Marriages and careers are sometimes tragically affected by this bad habit. You may have viewed procrastination as a personal problem that affected only your life. But it is important for you to accept responsibility for the way your behavior inconveniences or hurts others. Here is how you can accept responsibility for the results of your behavior and make amends:

- Consider each area of activity where you have procrastinated in the past. For each part of your life (work, school, family, friendships, and so on) consider the people whose lives touch yours, and identify how your procrastination has affected them.
- Admit to yourself that, even though you are not purposely inconveniencing others, your lack of action may have negative consequences in others' lives.
- Acknowledge any regret you feel over how your procrastination habit has negatively affected others. Communicate your regrets to

PROCRASTINATION

those who have been negatively affected. For example, say, "I'm sorry I am late. I'm having a problem with time management, and I'm sincerely sorry for any inconvenience this caused you." If you feel uncomfortable saying this directly, send your regrets in a note.

- Whenever possible, make amends to correct any problems you have caused. For example, if the mail in your office doesn't get out on time because you procrastinated, make amends by going out of your way to drive to the post office. That way you take the consequences rather than make others pay the price for the effects of your behavior.

List all the people you can think of who have been negatively affected or inconvenienced by the consequences of your procrastination:

1. _____
2. _____
3. _____
4. _____
5. _____
6. _____
7. _____
8. _____
9. _____
10. _____

Acknowledge to them any regret you feel for having caused them inconvenience because of your problem with procrastination. After you have done so, place a check mark next to their names.

Make amends whenever possible, except when to do so would cause further problems for others. After you have done all you can do, cross each name off the list.

THE EMOTIONAL FREEDOM WORKBOOK

Congratulations! You've completed Part 4 of *The Emotional Freedom Workbook*. Take a moment to write out the three most valuable lessons you've learned about freedom from procrastination.

1. _____

2. _____

3. _____

Celebrating Your Success

Since we have such a huge crowd of men of faith watching us from the grandstands, let us strip off anything that slows us down or holds us back, and especially those sins that wrap themselves so tightly around our feet and trip us up; and let us run with patience the particular race that God has set before us.—Hebrews 12:1 TLB

By completing *The Emotional Freedom Workbook,* you have done your best to honestly evaluate your life and take action to improve your condition. You should already be noticing significant improvements. Most of all, you deserve to be applauded for exercising your faith, moving ahead when you might have felt hopeless, and exhibiting the courage you needed to get the job done. All that's left for you to do is to evaluate your success. You may not be perfectly happy, but you should be able to see your way clear to know what the path to a healthier and happier future looks like.

Answer these questions about working through this book:

How has your physical health improved? _____
_____

How has your mental attitude changed for the better? _____
_____

How has your spiritual life changed for the better? _____

_____

How has your emotional well-being improved? _____

_____

How have specific relationships within your family improved?

_____

How have friendships changed for the better?_____

_____

What new information did you learn that opened up new possibilities for you?

_____

_____

How have your attitudes become more positive? _____

_____

How have you become more understanding of your condition?

_____

What have you discovered about yourself that pleased you?

_____

What commitments have you made that will help you live a healthier life?

_____

What resources are you aware of that you were not aware of before?

_____

CELEBRATING YOUR SUCCESS

List the key things you have learned about yourself: _____

_____

_____

_____

_____

_____

_____

List the life changes you have made:_____

_____

_____

_____

_____

_____

_____

List the areas of interest you have discovered:_____

_____

_____

_____

_____

_____

_____

How do you feel different about yourself and your lifestyle now that you have completed *The Emotional Freedom Workbook*? _____

_____

_____

_____

_____

How do you intend to celebrate the completion of the workbook (you may want to include your workbook companion in the celebration!)?

_____

_____

Remember, one day at a time:

- Keep your dreams clearly in sight.
- Keep your goals well defined.
- Keep your tasks identified.
- Keep your obstacles targeted for attack.
- Keep your relationships growing.

The Lord be with you!

About the Authors

Stephen Arterburn is cofounder and chairman of the New Life Clinics, one of the largest Christian counseling services in the United States. He is currently cohost of the New Life Clinic radio program with a listening audience of more than one million. He is a nationally known speaker and has been a regular guest on nationally syndicated television talk shows. He is the author or coauthor of more than twenty books, including *Winning at Work Without Losing at Love, The Angry Man, Addicted to "Love,"* and *The Power Book.* Arterburn holds degrees from Baylor University and the University of North Texas and has been awarded two honorary doctorate degrees. In 1993 he was named Socially Responsible Entrepreneur of the Year by *Inc. Magazine,* Ernst and Young, and Merrill Lynch. Arterburn and his wife, Sandy, and daughter, Madeline, live in Laguna Beach, California.

If you are interested in having Stephen Arterburn speak to your organization or at a special event, please contact:

Stephen Arterburn
P.O. Box 5009
Laguna Beach, CA 92651

714-376-0707
714-494-1272 FAX

For assistance with personal or emotional problems, call the New Life Clinics at 1-800-NEW-LIFE.

Connie Neal is a gifted writer and speaker who is committed to biblical truth and displays a unique talent for applying God's Word to real-life situations. She is the author or coauthor of twenty-six books including *Dancing in the Arms of God,* is a contributor to *The Women's Devotional Bible II,* and is associate editor of *The Life Recovery Bible.*

Books by Stephen Arterburn

Addicted to "Love" (Servant)

The Angry Man, Arterburn and David Stoop (Word)

The Complete Life Encyclopedia, Arterburn, Frank Minirth, M.D., and Paul Meier, M.D. (Thomas Nelson)

Drug-Proof Your Kids, Arterburn and Jim Burns (Focus on the Family; re-released by Gospel Light)

Faith That Hurts, Faith That Heals (originally titled *Toxic Faith*) Arterburn and Jack Felton (Thomas Nelson)

52 Simple Ways to Say "I Love You," Arterburn and Carl Dreizler (Thomas Nelson)

Gentle Eating, Arterburn, Mary Ehemann, and Vivian Lamphear, Ph.D. (Thomas Nelson)

Gentle Eating Workbook, Arterburn and Vivian Lamphear, Ph.D. (Thomas Nelson)

Growing Up Addicted (Ballantine)

Hand-Me-Down Genes and Second-Hand Emotions (hardcover: Thomas Nelson; paperback as *Hand Me Down Genes:* Simon & Schuster)

How Will I Tell My Mother?, Arterburn and Jerry Arterburn (Thomas Nelson)

The Life Recovery Bible, Arterburn and David Stoop, executive editors (Tyndale)

Miracle Drugs, Arterburn, Frank Minirth, M.D., and Paul Meier, M.D. (Thomas Nelson)

The Power Book, (Thomas Nelson)

The 12 Step Life Recovery Devotional, Arterburn and David Stoop (Tyndale)

When Love Is Not Enough, Arterburn and Jim Burns (hardcover and paperback as *Steering Them Straight:* Focus on the Family)

When Someone You Love Is Someone You Hate, Arterburn and David Stoop (Word)

Winning at Work Without Losing at Love (Thomas Nelson)

If you can't find one of these books in your local bookstore, you can order it through 1-800-BOOKS45.

To purchase the Finding the Power to Win audio and video series, phone 1-800-528-3825.

Printed in the United States
123746LV00002B/133-172/A